CREDIB
CONFIDENCE

How to Leverage PR as a Start-up

By Abbi E. Hoxleigh

To Elke
Onwards + Upwards
Abbi x

Book Cover Design: Deearo Marketing
Editor: Laura Billingham
Typesetting: Nicola Matthews
Publishing: Sharon Brown

THE BOOK CHIEF
IGNITE YOUR WRITING

TABLE OF CONTENTS

CHAPTER 11 161

MAINTAINING YOUR ENERGY AND FOCUS................................... 161

CHAPTER 12 175

YOUR EXPERT BREAKTHROUGH 175

DEDICATION

Dedicated to my parents, Pauline and Peter Head.

I know that wherever you are, you are proud of me and always have been.

BUILD YOUR BRAND REPUTATION

The words and actions of everyone in your company reflect on the CEO, organisation and stakeholders

For every organisation, effective communication is critical. It builds a solid reputation that protects you when things go wrong. With so many media channels, news spreads instantly; therefore, CEOs and their employees need to become more conscious of how they're perceived. Anyone can share every message, tweet or email with millions of people worldwide before you know what has happened. Working with a PR and communications strategist enables you to avoid PR pitfalls as a start-up, SME or non-profit. Public relations can help you to ethically curate your digital footprint and gain a legacy of earned and paid media coverage that increases customer trust. Effectively combining media channels and providing thought leadership content with a sense of social purpose shows your authority and go-to expertise. In the grip of a company crisis, brand reputation is crucial. Authentically communicating your vision with your team then to your customers beforehand creates a crisis buffer on which you can rely. That means getting the right PR support for your business brand at the right time.

Abbi Head, founder of Little PR Rock Marketing, came second in the Public Relations Today Most Valuable Post (MVP) Awards 2022 and is also a Member of the Chartered Institute of Public Relations.

● Book a free one-hour PR online consultation or meeting in person at the University of Warwick.
E: *abbi@littleprrockmarketing.co.uk*
littleprrockmarketing.co.uk

LITTLE **PR** ROCK

PRAISE FOR CREDIBILITY CONFIDENCE

"I love the way this book is written; it is definitely in Abbi's voice! It sounds authentic, passionate and has a clear empathy with clients. Abbi knows her stuff, and that comes out very clearly. The stories are so rich and reinforce her expertise and experience, helping to show who she is and what she is about. I really like the explanation of PR, and Abbi makes a great point about working with journalists. I like the quotes and references to other books, which all add credibility. I also love the models – they are really good at showing expertise in an easy way. Abbi shares some amazing advice on dealing with journalists, especially in chapter 4 – gold dust! I love her definition of a thought leader. It seems to me her book is useful for anyone wanting to do PR at any stage, not just start up."

Rachael McNidder

Director, Summit Human Potential

rachael@summit-humanpotential.com

www.summit-humanpotential.com

"With this book, Abbi demonstrates her understanding and depth of knowledge of the range of media, marketing, and public relations. Well written and informative. A must-read."

Marcus Grodentz

Motivational and Public Speaking Coach

novuslc@aol.com

novuslifecoaching.com

Marcus did his formal journalistic training on the Watford Observer and went to the journalism school at Harlow College – the same one attended by Piers Morgan. He worked for London News Service simultaneously as Anne Robinson and her then-husband-to-be John Penrose. He was Chief Reporter for the Lea Valley Mercury in Hertfordshire.

☆☆☆☆☆

"This book is a wonderful mix of anecdotes, lessons learned by someone who has newly established a PR agency, and advice on gaining media coverage. Abbi shares her experiences, good and bad, of moving from an in-house role as a media officer to becoming self-employed as a PR and Communications Strategist. Whilst she has achieved significant exposure for herself and her clients in a short time, Abbi gives the reader a thorough insight into the highs and lows of working with journalists. The book is ideal for new business owners but will also be of interest to entrepreneurs who have yet to discover the power of PR. By following Abbi's advice, all of us can gain media coverage, leverage our expertise, and build brand awareness of our businesses. Having worked in marketing communications for over 30 years, the book still delivered a fresh view of the industry and insightful observations. A must-read for anyone interested in taking their visibility to the next level."

Joanne Parker

Communications Specialist

joanne@jpwritingservices.co.uk

☆☆☆☆☆

"I absolutely love the chatty style and the positive affirmations for the reader throughout the book. It is informal, without being overdone. Abbi takes a lot of the technical 'jargon' out of the text to make it more accessible to the layperson. There is plenty of information here that I really would never have thought of. Abbi's life experiences make her very relatable and very endearing. I think the bit about writing your own book in Chapter 12 is well worded and great advice!"

Mark Elson, Beta Reader

FOREWORD

By Wendy Brown

As Abbi E. Hoxleigh's mentor at the Coventry and Warwickshire Chamber of Commerce, Wendy Brown has been her guiding star. After connecting at local business networking events, they met again in 2018 when Abbi joined one of the Chamber's fully funded workshops. These sessions include 1:1 business coaching and mentoring to help get business ideas up and running. The lessons stayed with Abbi over the years and created the foundations for Little PR Rock Marketing in 2020.

Abbi still refers to the business plan that Wendy helped her to create in one of her group sessions every time she needs to assess where she is at and what she is doing

These are Wendy's words…

"Credibility Confidence: How to Leverage PR as a Start-up is a great guide to what the hell public relations (PR) is and what it isn't. Abbi exposes the myths: that only large established businesses can afford to engage a PR consultant; and that new start-ups are not ready to join the club. As a business advisor who supported Abbi on her early start-up journey, she says it as it is. Within this book, Abbi shares her highs and lows, successes and failures, and how she continues to reach her goals and that of her clients through her determination and hard work. Her book is full of hints and tips on how to harness the power of getting your brand message heard and one every start-up should read."

Wendy

For more about similar courses:

Coventry & Warwickshire Chamber of Commerce

https://www.cw-chamber.co.uk/

INTRODUCTION

This book is filled with everything I've learned about PR as a start-up to help you understand what it can do for your business. Whilst there is plenty of tangible advice in the book, it is more than just a series of guides and templates. You'll learn how PR compares to traditional marketing and how it can elevate you and your business by turning you into a thought leader. You'll also find out some of the pitfalls I've made along the way when seeking media attention and get tips on creating your own content that journalists will notice. It is designed to offer a practical guide to PR strategy as it reflects my own experience. You will find your own path as you build credibility and learn to believe in yourself. This book is intended to give you some insight into my philosophy of PR and help you develop your own unique style. If it works for you, keep doing it; if not, try something else until you find the approach that fits your personality and goals. Finding your voice, becoming a rising star, and creating content that adds massive value are the first steps on the path to PR success.

I could tell you, "One morning in my first year as a start-up business, my company was featured in The Sunday Times, and that publicity generated 1,000 new leads and 150 new clients". You would likely be impressed. The truth is that it didn't happen. However, with public relations (PR) it could surprise you one day. It might just be unlikely for a start-up. If I had received 150 clients after being featured in the news back then, I would have been overwhelmed as a new business, panicked, and probably failed to deliver on my promises.

"What really happened that morning?" you may be asking. My alarm went off, and I sleepily leaned over to check my 42 emails scheduled the night before. There it was - like a golden ticket to Willy Wonka's chocolate factory - overnight, I had media coverage for a client in an industry magazine I was unfamiliar with. That is the nature of PR. There are no guarantees, and uncertainty becomes a way of life.

When I decided to write this book for you, I remembered the challenges I faced when I first started out in business and all the conflicting choices I was given to try and promote myself. I had been working as a Media Officer at an established charity for ten years, so you would think I should have a head start. During the COVID-19 lockdown of 2020, home-based duties as an employee created a work-life harmony for me, with extra hours in the day dedicated to self-improvement. I committed to developing a growth mindset and fast-tracking online public speaking and leadership skills.

I gained a sense of autonomy and increased confidence that prompted me to consider my potential to become self-employed as a PR professional. My identity shifted with additional expert support from life coaches and free training from many successful entrepreneurs, content creators, and presentation, PR, and marketing experts. I craved and crammed knowledge into the early hours of the morning. I had more time for networking and cut my teeth on the 10 -15-minute speaker slots with my presentation slide decks that I am remembered for. Before the pandemic, I was an introvert. Now I describe myself as a self-assured introvert who can confidently speak about PR and what has worked for me over the years.

When I stood on the stage at the Federation of Small Business (FSB) Business Bootcamp in March 2022 and delivered a talk on what I have learned about PR, I knew my experience could help others. That talk led to me being quoted as an expert in the organisation's *First Voice* magazine and gave me the confidence to speak on *Ticker News Insights* about my journey. I call this process of building media coverage and visibility 'Stacking', and it has been something I developed when I began as a start-up to gain credibility, boost my reputation, and build trust. Now I am mastering this rollercoaster of being seen as an authority and go-to expert or, in other words, my 'Credibility Confidence'. Hence the title of this first book.

I never felt like an expert, even though I have credentials, including a Chartered Institute of PR Membership, a Postgraduate Certificate in Creative Design, and many years of experience. Academic knowledge didn't give me the confidence I thought it would when I started out. I remember the first time I wrote for *Prowly*, a PR industry blog. When the article went live, I felt anxiety rise from my feet and take over my body. It made me feel light-headed and sick. I took an hour to calm down before reading the piece. PR is a shake-up of emotions that means you end up like Teflon - impervious to criticism and immune to failure.

My business is called Little PR Rock Marketing, and the letters PR also stands for perseverance and resilience. Now I channel my efforts into communication between my clients and the media. I focus on what we call 'earned media,' creating a balance between the stories my clients want to promote and the need for newsworthy content by the media.

As a publicist, I am in the middle, protecting the integrity of both sides. I like to see my clients in the press, on television, radio and in magazines in print or online, in fact, anywhere where I know their ideas will be heard. I help my clients develop a positive digital footprint and create a legacy of media coverage that impacts this world. All it takes is a great idea, the problem you have solved for a group of people as a start-up. The rest is your business destiny as you navigate the ups and downs of building your empire.

AS SEEN IN

St James's Place

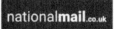

Prowly
A Semrush Company

nationalmail.co.uk

BUSINESS MONDAYS.

Warwickshire World

PRmoment

fsb

ValiantCEO

Entrepreneur Tribune

MO2VATE

go to yellow

RUGBY Radio

bbpmedia

Authority Magazine

THE BUSINESS GROWTH NETWORK

ticker NEWS

© 2021 www.johnclearyphotography.co.uk

22

CHAPTER 1

The Fundamentals of PR

It's Time to Change the Way You Think About Public Relations

There's a lot of emphasis on the glamorous side of PR: the red carpet, the fancy events, and the VIP access. However, PR for a start-up is less about publicity and more about developing your reputation internally and externally. This includes what I call your 'Internal Reputation Compass', or how you see your own credibility, and alternatively, your 'External Reputation Standards', or how others come to recognise and trust you. PR is essentially about communication with your stakeholders, which is anyone who has an interest in your business. For example, that could be your customers, suppliers, investors, employees, or stockists. It's an extension of the work you're already doing to engage with your audience.

PR is how you connect with your stakeholders and help them understand why they should continue to pay attention to you. That could be because you have something to say that's interesting or because you're the kind of person who has something to offer - your expertise on a subject is valuable enough for people to want to keep informed about what you have to say.

PR is also about making yourself available and approachable, which means being open to answering questions and interacting with people who aren't necessarily paying customers yet. The more established you get with your audience, the more willing they'll be to buy from you - but they won't do so without knowing what they're getting first. That means not just showing them what you do but showing them why they should care enough to spend money on it.

Over the past few years, there's been a lot of talk about how to reach the media. But it's not just about getting our name in print or on air; it's about how we can do that in meaningful and effective ways. For example, I worked with a client who has a CIC charity; we helped her gain television exposure when she spoke about a topic that was getting massive media attention. Working with her was one of my favourite projects to date because it was so gratifying to see her speaking passionately on television news about her new venture.

Where are you starting with your PR journey?

When people find information about you in newspapers, radio, magazines, websites, television, or any other form of media, they are more likely to believe it. Your PR lets the media tell your story for you and embellishes it with journalists' insights and interpretations. This indirect and independent third-party endorsement is the value of PR, and I focus on earning that valuable media coverage for my clients. How do you feel about your own credibility? How do people talk about you when you are not there? When you Google yourself, what do you see? These are questions that I ask myself regularly. I have overcome challenges that I can now talk about freely. It wasn't always that way. I say that PR can take your reputation personally and professionally from "Zero to Hero" because that is my own experience, as you will see in Chapter 2.

Why PR is essential for any business, no matter the size

The more you know about PR as a start-up, the better equipped you are to help craft your image and tackle your PR without spin. When you control your brand message in your marketing, you're the one telling people about your incredible products and services. As a result, you control how people see your brand, whether that's attracting customers or repelling them.

Alternatively, earned PR is when someone other than you amplifies your consistent brand message and boosts your reputation and credibility. For my clients and for me, PR is about building trust and becoming a go-to expert on a subject. The role of the media in our lives is constantly evolving, and now more than ever, we're all aware that we need to be smart about how we deal with them. We want to share our stories and experiences with a wide audience who will appreciate what we have to say. We don't want to waste journalists' time, or our own, by pitching something that isn't relevant or interesting, and we certainly don't want to burn our bridges by acting unprofessionally.

As a start-up, PR is the most cost-effective way to get your personal brand in front of your target audience. It is a great way to build positive relationships with customers. When your audience sees the publicity you have earned from PR, rather than the advertising messages you pay for and promote yourself, they are more likely to trust you. By building a brand with a strong personality and communicating what you stand for, you build upon that trust with your customers. Brand integrity and consistency are essential to your PR, marketing, and advertising campaigns. PR is your credibility and the respect and recognition it brings you. It is your reputation - which cannot be bought. The sense of satisfaction that comes from being featured in a reputation-building piece can be extremely rewarding.

Turn your marketing into a PR message

A very dear client of mine recently gained a potential BBC radio interview about her matchmaking business. When I first spoke to her, I suggested that we pitch about her in-person singles night events. She began to tell me everything she needed to include from her own marketing message, but then I asked her to summarise these points for me in one sentence and change her focus.

"Can I stop you there?" I asked. "Let's talk about the COVID-19 lockdown, how we have forgotten body language, our unrealistic expectations of starting relationships, the effects of programmes we watch on television such as Love Island and Married at First Sight." This proved to be an effective strategy because she began to look through the lens of a journalist. Her first words still make me smile. "Why are we talking about all that?" The explanation is that she's not trying to promote a product but rather make news by discussing something topical. Being interviewed on the radio as an 'expert' in her field for her opinions gives her a credible presence, making her argument convincing enough for listeners to think about her offers.

Establishing a PR strategy which positions you as an expert in your field gives you authenticity and accountability that you can align with your social purpose. When challenges affect the perception of your brand, and they will at some point, people will be more likely to forgive you because their trust in your company is already established.

As time passes, you will thrive with your business, establish your reputation, and earn the trust of others. You may gain new customers through unexpected channels and reinvent or pivot as you develop your offerings and pricing. Your PR efforts will become intertwined with your company and offer opportunities to build a niche brand identity and subject-matter expertise. Your values will influence potential customers' buying decisions. Scott Baradell, CEO at Idea Grove, states that your products and services are the body of your business, your social purpose is its heart, and thought leadership is its mind. When all three are in place, it creates a positive force.

How PR is the use of 'earned media'

PR is about more than just reaching out to newspapers with press releases and pitching. It can be other engagements, such as speaking opportunities, guest posting, your responses to your social media, event management, market research, networking, and crisis management. Crisis communication is something of a skill in itself for when things go wrong or for what I call a 'Damage Limitation'.

For me, PR is about great storytelling. As a qualified graphic designer, I used to tell stories through images and text. I also learned the art of written communication as an academic and charity Media Officer for ten years. I learned how words can change perception while still maintaining my integrity. People are often sceptical about marketing because the message is purposely persuasive. To get technical, in our marketing we often use 'paid media' (advertisements) or `owned media.' (websites, newsletters, emails etc.) In comparison, any publicity you have not created or paid for is called 'earned media' or can be 'shared media' such as our social media.

GINI DEITRICH

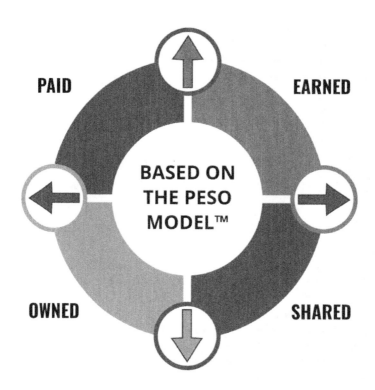

PAID

EARNED

BASED ON
THE PESO
MODEL™

OWNED

SHARED

The key to PR is getting as much positive media exposure for yourself as possible. That means knowing where your name should be and when, where, and how it should be presented. You will try to acquire positive, technically correct, engaging coverage that is also fair. However, many people believe they can 'control' their image by controlling what media they appear in. Many media outlets will accept certain amounts of control from contributors, but in the end, the media make all the decisions about what to publish and air. The key to success is knowing when to take a backseat and when it's okay to stand out.

Examples of PR tools include:

- Press releases
- Speaking engagements
- Pitching to journalists
- Networking
- Guest posting
- Social media responses
- Event management
- Market research
- Crisis management etc

Build media relationships with impact

For me, good PR is about building mutually beneficial relationships with journalists, editors, producers, or other media members, but most importantly, with your audience. I use a process I call the 'Impactful Media Relationship Builder.' However, I just want to stress that it doesn't matter who you know if you don't have a great story.

IMPACTFUL MEDIA RELATIONSHIP BUILDER©

I ntelligent

M eaningful

P ersonal

A uthentic

C onversational

T imely

Your connection to the media needs to be intelligent and provide valuable commentary, insights, news, and tips that are well-grounded and have substance. Your relationship with the media then becomes meaningful and has value beyond promotion to provide audiences with the reality of life and experience on a deeper level. Taking a personal approach to communications with the media means you respect their role and are not using them for free publicity. This way, when you approach the media, your response will be authentic and conversational rather than one-sided and self-driven. The most important thing is timely communication. When you land in the journalists' inbox, the way you hook their attention will be the game-changer.

The question becomes: how do I make this email welcome in the journalist's inbox? In other words, how do you not automatically end up in a spam folder? Or worse, have your email opened and all your further correspondence added to their spam folder?

When dealing with the media, you must be strategic about approaching them. You can't just blast out a press release or email asking for coverage. That's self-promotion, and it doesn't get you anywhere; it makes the journalist think you're only in it for yourself, not for generating good content. It also makes them feel like they have more work to do sifting through your promotional stuff to find the bits they actually care about. This isn't just a one-sided relationship; you have to respect the role they play and not use them as a platform for shameless self-promotion. If you take a personal approach to communicating with the media, your response will feel more natural. Respect their role and don't take advantage of it.

There are no guarantees in all media coverage; often, it is an "earned" inclusion. I learned quickly that journalists might love my ideas for stories. They could be enthusiastic about featuring my clients or me in their publications, so I would tell my client, "The journalist really liked it!" and they would get excited too. Suddenly there was a challenge ahead; the journalist needed to get approval from their editor, producer or someone overseeing them. So, I would wait while they pitched the idea to them.

Despite the excitement, there may be no further response or reaction, and the journalist might become difficult to contact. I describe this as 'Crickets', an idiom I have adopted from the influx of webinars I have seen from the United States. I would then realise the editor or producer had not loved the story quite as much, and there would not be a feature for my client. That was a hard conversation I had a few times to let my clients down. So, rather than getting excited on that first contact, I learned to sit on this knowledge until I was absolutely sure my hard work had paid off; that I had gained success. I realised why my role was all about communication between the client promoting themselves and the journalist looking for a story.

Thought leadership is not 'PR Spin'

Unfortunately for me, PR is often seen as a sales-generating machine. While it certainly serves that function for some companies, it's not the primary function of PR, which is a strategic tool used to build relationships with stakeholders and earn their trust. PR is all about investment in 'The Long Game.' I need to know that my clients are ready for the peaks and valleys of PR before they work with me.

You need to ask yourself too. You may be more ready than you think. How I work with my business owner clients involves finding the core messages relevant to their industry as a subject matter expert or potentially a thought leader. My process includes 'thought leadership marketing'. You can do that, too, because PR is about finding time, not money.

You may have heard the term 'spin' as it relates to PR. But what does it mean? Spin is often referred to as "the art of making news" or even "the dark art of PR." It's when you take an event that is bad for your business and manipulate it into something positive. In other words, spin is considered lying. Spin can damage your business' reputation when it goes wrong because it can show people that you are dishonest. It's important to be as open and transparent as possible; your customers will appreciate it and be much more receptive to your PR efforts because you'll seem more trustworthy. If you're caught using spin, people will start questioning everything else you say, which can lead to a major PR blunder. Once spin was just told verbally, but now with technology, spin can be spread faster than ever before and can have an incredibly damaging effect on someone's reputation. The reality is that, at worst, the ultimate goal of good PR must be to ethically nudge public opinions to change through a strategic message, not to hide the truth.

Find your unmissable news stories

As a start-up, you'll have to wear many hats. One of those hats is PR. That's why it's important to plan ahead and not wait until your business grows before you start thinking about the best way to manage your PR campaigns. When you're starting out, you have more time to learn the PR ropes, keep up with trends, plan ahead, and use the free services available to you as you grow. If you're in the planning stages and thinking about expanding your business, consider how you can take advantage of every cost-effective PR tool available such as the ones I mention in Chapter 3. When you have customers, you may find that scaling your business is time-consuming. A PR professional can help you to increase your visibility in the marketplace, and you will have the experience to help them to do their job better.

PR practitioners know how to select stories that are likely to be written and let go of those stories that never will be. As a client, release yourself of concerns that your news release will be rewritten before it is published. The risks are worth the rewards. There is sometimes an element of fear involved with the unknown, but journalists and editors generally report honestly on the products and services they write about. They want to get it right and are more likely to be truthful in their writing if they know they can trust the sources they're working with.

At Little PR Rock Marketing, we use a combination of PR and marketing to help business owners and professionals, consultants, entrepreneurs, authors, and speakers gain Credibility Confidence as subject-matter experts and developing thought leaders. To "earn media", I ask my clients to think on the next level to up their marketing game. To get media attention, you need to convince them to feature a positive story about you, your brand, or your issue. Remember that editorial features have more credibility because they are often independently verified by a trusted third party rather than purchased.

Do you have a newsworthy story that is a game-changer to challenge traditional views of your industry? Do you have up-to-date insights to share that resonate with your target audience in a way that they need to hear about? If so, you need to ask yourself whether this is the right time to market your message through PR. At an online event, I spoke about PR, and the group was asked to talk about their perception of what PR is and what it means to them in their business before I spoke. I was not shocked by the answers since many people understood PR can cover many areas of marketing. Though I was disappointed to think that many people thought PR was advertising. Thankfully, I was heartened to discover that one member understood the process for creating an advertorial; an advertorial is formed as half editorial, half paid advertisement. There is more to come on advertorials in Chapter 6.

Introducing 'The 5 Key ROI Marketing Principles©

My PR strategy is driven by the desire to help your business become the best it can be so you will be noticed. I spent ten years working in media for a charity before becoming a PR professional, so my perspective differs from those who have previously worked in journalism. My PR/ Marketing strategy is based on my own, called The Five Key ROI Marketing Principles©. These include Respect, Recognition, Resilience, Reputation and Reinforcement on Investment. This is a nod to the term 'return on investment (ROI)' which is one of the most difficult things to measure in PR. It's a hard metric to set for PR, as every brand and product is different. However, there are some things we can learn from the past and apply to the future. For more detail about the Five Key ROI Marketing Principles, see Chapter 11.

PR has come a long way from the days of sending out press releases and hoping they get picked up by a few media outlets. With social media, PR has become more interactive with the consumer and specifically targeted at the individual or company.

As start-ups, it is easy to forget we possess valuable expertise and a sense of humour. The serious side of business can keep us tethered to a professional image in person and online. Some people like me are super professional and fail miserably, like Bridget Jones. I think that "messy and authentic" behaviour comes with the territory for start-ups; it is part of what makes us feel like imposters when we run our businesses. Although I have been knocked back a few times, I have managed to master my inner critic. As I said to my friend over coffee, "My self-belief has not caught up with my increased abilities yet"; this means that I am still reactive and only 'unconsciously competent.' I have been a start-up, too, so I know that imposter syndrome is a constant battle.

Before you spend big on marketing, make sales first

Your first order of business when starting a new business is not getting business cards or hiring a PR firm. It is not finding the perfect domain name or figuring out what kind of logo you want. The most important thing you can do for yourself is to start generating sales. It's easy to feel that you somehow look unprofessional if you don't have a logo or business cards or if your website is a template with stock photos. It seems like the right thing to do is to try and present yourself as a serious company with an official presence.

I can't overstate how wrong I have discovered this attitude to be. Not only does it drain your resources and distract you from more important things, but it's also the wrong way to create a professional image for yourself.

When you start out, it's important to identify your target audience, how to reach them, and how to build a reputation. Once you have proof of your concept, you can use your free time to focus on aligning your marketing efforts with PR. You will also have the data to determine how much attention is needed to grow your business by knowing what it takes to attract, convert, and retain them as customers.

My point of view aligns with Alan Dibb's book called 'The One Page Marketing Plan'. Marketing through brand recognition is better suited to major brands as it demands a saturation level to penetrate your audience's consciousness. Start-ups often don't have the budget or time to run promotions in sufficient quantities to impact their target audiences. Their attempts to gain visibility are like a drop in the ocean. It's nowhere near enough to reach the consciousness of their target market, which is bombarded by thousands of marketing messages each day. So, start-ups get drowned out and see little or no return on investment (ROI).

I started Little PR Rock Marketing with a limited budget, no business cards, subscriptions, or a Customer Relations Manager (CRM). Just me, gaining knowledge and providing skills swaps, discounts, and freebies to establish what clients need. I found PR opportunities that were free and boosted my confidence. Now I have retainer clients, have become an educational public speaker and trainer, scaling up my business and am featured or quoted in magazines in print and online.

Don't settle for anything less than amazing

Being considered an expert isn't as out of reach or as responsible as it sounds. It can be a lot of fun, and you'll find the more you do it, the more comfortable it will feel. Here's how to start gaining 'Credibility Confidence' with this new PR role in your life:

- Know why you're doing it.
- Be prepared for what will happen next
- Get ready to potentially 'eat your words'
- Find people you trust who can help you.
- Start small and work up to bigger projects.

CHAPTER 2

Reputation is a Gamechanger

Trust Is Like Oxygen. You Need It and Don't Even Know It

"We don't want you here."

When I returned to my hometown after my darkest time at university, my reputation was absolutely zero. At the time, it felt like that would never end. I can remember arriving at a nightclub to meet old friends and being told at the door that I was not welcome. When I returned home, I felt upset and confused; however, I was determined to overcome the rejection.

Since then, I have worked on my mindset and personal brand, created a business and spoken about my expertise in PR with confidence and clarity. With a diagnosis of Post-traumatic stress disorder (PTSD), I still get flashbacks of a time when I was on medication that stiffened my joints and when my tongue curled. My arms were locked at 90 degrees, making communication almost impossible. Now communication is the essence of what I do every day, and those times are far behind me. I use communication to learn, discern, and share helpful information.

In 2022 I stepped up as a Media Volunteer for the charity Rethink Mental Illness, separately from my PR business. Rethink's goal is to ensure everyone affected by mental illness has a good quality of life. When I joined as a Media Volunteer, I knew it did not matter if I felt 'uncomfortable' if just one person benefited from what I shared for Rethink. I decided that after 30 years, I can talk about:

- Finding a path through education and employment is possible for someone with PTSD and a diagnosis of Bipolar
- How the rollercoaster of Bipolar experiences in my life has dragged my moods with it
- Why my experiences working as a Community Mental Health Worker in a Rethink recovery house changed my opinions on mental health provision
- What I call the 'Organic Psychosis Assumption' and how many people have relied on that initial labelling unnecessarily
- The state of in-patient care and protecting vulnerable patients while they are in hospital

So why am I telling you this? Knowing what you have to offer the media and when it comes from a place of sincerity is key to gaining trust. I could tell you more about my experiences being a Rethink Media Volunteer, but it would not be relevant to this book. This book is about your PR as a start-up business. This story is to show you how as a start-up, you can go from 'Zero to Hero' in making an impact regardless of where you start personally or professionally.

How to use "The Source Trust Triangle©"

Would you listen if I could tell you five ways I managed to bounce back into being an educational speaker from that painful rejection at the nightclub? If so, it is probably because you trust my opinion based on what you know about me so far. You are beginning to trust me. The media are no different. A journalist is looking for credibility in your story, so I developed the 'Source Trust Triangle©' to remind me to stay focused on becoming a trusted source of information.

THE SOURCE TRUST TRIANGLE©

INTEGRITY

BENEFITS

QUALIFIED

RELIABLE

TRUST

SOURCE

Over the years, I have included this in my daily habits. You may want to write down these six key elements of the triangle to help you remember them:

- Integrity as one of your values

- Benefits of what you can share

- Qualification or demonstration of ability to provide the information

- Reliability so that media can come back to you again and again

- Trust and building relationships

- Enjoy adding value

You will become an accessible, trusted source of information when you have integrity, can demonstrate the benefits of what you have to say, and are qualified with the experience and knowledge to back up your insights and opinion. Trust is so important when it comes to the reputation of a business. It is not just journalists' trust you need to gain. If a customer does not trust a business and does not like or agree with the products or services they sell, they will not be likely to buy from them. A lack of trust can also affect a company's ability to attract and retain employees.

Find your voice, find your core values

Three key values have been at the core of my business. They are integrity, transparency, and loyalty. Doing business with integrity means being true to myself and being honest, upright, and decent by fulfilling my obligations, following my conscience, and sticking by my principles. These have been crucial to my PR journey. When volunteering at The New Art Gallery Walsall in the UK, I raised my hand at a conference with an opinion that felt true to my principles. It required confidence to be bold, yet I needed to speak up. Now I am an educational and inspirational public speaker who can motivate an audience because of my point of view.

I have been transparent throughout my life as a PR and Communications Strategist. When I own up to the mistakes I have made and the setbacks I have faced, I can better assess the situation and prevent similar errors. I am always upfront with my customers but do not reveal proprietary information that would give competitors an unfair advantage. Loyalty is essential to protect your own reputation and that of those you are associated with. Without loyalty, our PR relationships can seem one-sided and cannot develop. As a start-up, these three values are very important to develop your PR strategy because the path is not smooth.

'Marketing With Perseverance and Resilience' is my tagline because I believe business owners should not give up on their ventures at the first hurdle. Examining the bigger picture, I try every solution until I have exhausted all my ideas. If that does not resolve the issue, I take a mental break, return to thinking more creatively and try again. Perseverance has been intrinsic to my professional and personal lives. I have needed to persevere through emotional health crises, build a resilient personal brand despite swimming upstream and achieve my professional qualifications.

Why we should take the leap into public relations

So now that I have told you a snippet of my story and my values, you may see my integrity and qualification and trust me even further. So, what is the best way to earn trust? It is to trust yourself, and you will learn that through personal development. Your personal development is essential because it keeps you accountable. It is about stepping out of your 'comfort zone'. I left employment after ten years as a Media Officer with a charity working in communications, appreciating that the "comfort zone" I was in is called that for a reason because it's 'comfortable'. There are many ways your insights will be formed from those you spend the most time around. It's critical for any business owner to be well informed about the industry in which they operate; it's a matter of survival. Your PR is affected by how you see your Credibility Confidence as a trusted source of information.

Here are 5 strategies to elevate yourself and your business

1. **Remember, PR requires a skill set and mindset of its own**

   When trying to get your idea or product out there, the last thing you need is a lack of confidence in your abilities. This is especially true when it comes to media comments. There's nothing more damaging than saying something and immediately realising it wasn't very well thought out. It makes you look bad on two levels; you look naive for saying it, and it makes you look like you haven't done your homework.

   Building knowledge and information is so important to improve your conceptual understanding. You can do this through goal setting and assessing your audience and customers' needs. You may attend interactive workshops, courses, and study groups. Every day you need to learn, trust yourself to understand what your new knowledge means to you and your business, and then apply it. Only when you are confident enough to say you have evidence can you confidently make media comments. If you have doubts, they will show, affecting how you are perceived.

2. **Learn about others' best practices, methods, and tools to gain clarity**

Observing models and examples is a way to learn from the past experiences of others so you don't have to go through them yourself. If you're thinking about starting your own business, it could save you time and money if you've already seen how another company handles certain issues. There are many ways you may form insights from those you spend the most time around. You can make visits or arrange meetings to observe how others manage their businesses, do peer observations, or take heed of their processes and systems. The most important thing is to watch and listen. Interestingly listening to people makes them trust you more too.

3. Include ongoing reflective practice for your business knowledge

Reflective practice in your business knowledge is essential. Taking time out to see what you have learned and achieved will make you more confident about taking new directions. You may keep journals that report on your everyday activities, keep a blog to return to, or use reflection tools to help you analyse what you need going forward. Reflective practice in business is the process of reviewing past experiences and events in order to improve future outcomes. It involves stepping back from the daily tasks of running a business and reflecting on how they are being carried out. This enables you to evaluate actions, clarify goals and objectives, assess performance, identify improvement opportunities, and develop future strategies.

Truly effective reflective practice can be difficult because it requires a certain amount of detachment from the daily pressures of business life. It takes dedication and discipline to take time out of your working schedule to think about what has gone well and where improvements can be made. It also requires taking a step back from the day-to-day activity of running a business so you can look at things as a whole rather than through the myopic lens of individual tasks or projects. Reflective practice requires you to make time for it.

4. **The impact of these 2 steps on your focus can be a game-changer**

When you're constantly learning, translating your new discoveries and insights into action will continue to be challenging. Two things I have learned have changed the way I look at my professional life. First, it is important to change my business practices to align them with the result I want to deliver. The second is that it is essential to reassess my relationships to align them with the way I want to be perceived by others.

In PR, it is important to associate yourself with people who share your integrity and values. That way, you share the trust. Once you can assess what needs to change and what needs to be done, you can make plans and take action more quickly. Changing your relationships means making changes in your professional network, who you spend time with, who writes about you or features you on their website or in their publication. You need to get people who will help create a true story for you or deliver news about your work and achievements into positions where they can help promote and advocate for your work.

5. **Use your expertise to help others without charging for your services**

I've been putting a lot of thought into how I can share my skills and knowledge for the benefit of both the PR industry and myself. While I have been sharing my knowledge and skills for free or, on many occasions, as a token gift, I've also spent time learning from others willing to share their wisdom. Instead of exchanging monies, I prefer to exchange in a way that's mutually beneficial. For example, when I first started as an independent consultant, I was willing to offer my services for free and was able to learn something from the client.

I'm a big believer in reciprocity and have often offered my services for free or as part of a time-banking or skills-swapping project. In addition to learning from others, I've also learned throughout my career that gaining shared experiences has been something that has spring boarded new avenues for my personal development and my PR business. This is where I focus my attention on the media. Continuing to refine instructional practice, sharing my wisdom, planning with my team, and sharing with my peers, mentoring, and networking are expanding my knowledge and the potential for my business.

Navigate with your "Internal Reputation Compass"

'Continuous Professional Development (CPD)' is not just a tool to keep track of your skills, knowledge, and experience. It informs your perception of yourself and becomes your 'Internal Reputation Compass'. In this way, keeping a record of your professional achievements is an advantage. You can regularly ask yourself questions such as:

- What did you learn last week?
- What did you learn this month or last month?
- What did you learn in the last year?

- How will this information be useful for you in the future?
- Will it help you improve your business or get a better job?
- Do you think it may be useful for other people as well?

If the answer to the last question is "yes", then you have a good reason to keep on tracking and monitoring your skills, knowledge, and experience for PR purposes. That is the content the media are looking for. The information is not only beneficial for you, but it can also help those around you.

Understand how you are driven to be an action-taker

Capability, Creation, Commitment, and Action are the four key ingredients for transforming your knowledge into real-world results. So, how do you leverage your existing knowledge to use in new situations? The Action Overlap Model© (AOM) is a tool that can help you do just that. Take a breath as there is another diagram on its way.

THE ACTION OVERLAP MODEL©

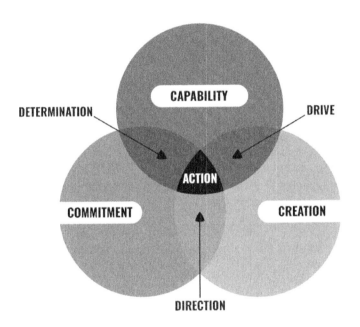

CREDIBILITY CONFIDENCE: How to Leverage PR as a Start-Up.

This model provides a visual representation of how people use their knowledge to inform their plans and how the overlap of these three elements - Capability, Creation and Commitment - creates the impetus to take action. It also illustrates how, without all three of them, there is no action.

Your actions and reactions can impact your reputation in a world of constant connectivity. Demonstrating your ability to think strategically with confidence and show leadership will build trust. When you are in the moment, it's important to stay committed to the task. If you act without consideration for what could happen due to that action, you are at risk of having to deal with the aftermath. You cannot underestimate the importance of learning. These are the following benefits for start-ups:

- skills and knowledge
- confidence in making decisions
- motivation as part of a team or collaboration
- the ability to bring fresh insights and the latest thinking
- deep level understanding
- management of complexities and unusual scenarios

The secret benefits of an established reputation

People don't just buy products or services; they buy into an organisation. Today, with the trend towards social media and personalisation, they also buy into the people behind the company - particularly the Chief Executive Officer (CEO). As a start-up, you are the CEO of your business as well as all the other hats you wear. As a start-up, trusting in your leadership from the onset is crucial. Your branding is about your personality and the traits transpose onto your business.

When you build a personal brand that is reliable and robust, you can be consistent in your interactions with customers and quickly become familiar with them. This consistency will build trust among your target audience, allowing an emotional connection between your personal brand and customers. This is an asset and a commodity you can rely on in a crisis. There is more on crisis management in Chapter 8 and 10.

During the COVID-19 pandemic, I learned that CEOs must have a strong voice and stand for something so that people can rely on them to speak for them. I learned the importance of honesty, humanity, and patience. I learned how important it is to keep all stakeholders informed in communications: silence is not an option. You need to develop a personal brand that includes keeping your audience well-informed and showing how you can use facts and figures, and anecdotes to support your points. I also recommend plain speaking without jargon and being transparent about questions you might be asked. By providing a no-nonsense personal brand, you will answer the brief perfectly.

The tone matters, too; a big part is staying calm in the face of pressure. If you can show that you have a method for staying calm, stakeholders will be more likely to give you a second chance when things go wrong. Everyone needs a second chance sometimes, but those with an established reputation often get them more easily than those who don't yet have one. The CEO, who views 'social purpose' as a personal calling, not just a business model, will build respect and trust. Millennials, in particular, increasingly seek out brands with sustainable values; they're willing to pay more for their products because they align with their values. This trend affects all generations; it's not limited to younger people. In fact, there's evidence that companies that build 'social purpose' into their business models outperform the market. As your personal branding develops, trust behaves like glue binding customers to a company.

This will grab attention...and you should too!

With so much online information, today's consumers have a huge amount of power at their fingertips. They can choose to do business with a company (or not) based on how they feel about its brand reputation or that of the CEO. PR is about creating disruptive content and understanding how customers and stakeholders perceive a brand. We live in a world where everyone is a reporter on life experiences, including their relationship with brands. So, we need to create compelling and relevant personal brand stories that are authentic for their customers so they can compete for valuable attention, especially in a crisis.

CHAPTER 3

Unleash Your Emerging Potential

Thought Leaders Get Featured in The Media

Yes, you can help reporters as a subject-matter expert, make a difference, and create an impact in the media to benefit your business with free PR. Here's one way to get started. HARO (Help a Reporter Out) is a free service that connects journalists with sources. It's a win-win for everyone, and it works. You can sign up for a free subscription to HARO. When you do, you'll immediately start getting email requests from journalists in press, television, radio, and magazines in print and online. These emails will provide you with daily media coverage opportunities broken down by categories like business, lifestyle, technology, and healthcare. I have appeared in interviews, articles, and blogs about my work via HARO.

Another great alternative for me has been the Twitter hashtag #journorequests. Journalists use social media rather like a search engine. You will find plenty of subscription sites, hashtags, and social media groups with pitch, press release or journalist request opportunities. Over the years, mine have included HARO, #journorequests, PressPlugs, PressLoft, Sourcebottle, several Facebook groups, and Journalism.co.uk, to name a few available. These are ideal places to master your pitches as a start-up. I have been as equally successful with these as I have faced crushing defeat. When replying to any journalist's email requests, my motto is to 'stay on the positive' and not be too controversial as a start-up until your reputation can manage the fallout.

How to pitch a news story in a fast-paced world

A PR pitch is a short message that outlines the value of a story and explains why it should be published. A good PR pitch should be persuasive, timely for the topic, and written in an engaging manner. When your story appears in print, online, or on television, you may get the kind of exposure that attracts new clients and customers, so it is worth learning how to pitch. However, pitching can be challenging. Add to this, the number of journalists is declining, faster news cycles demand more speed and efficiency from communicators, and there's an unprecedented number of media outlets to contend with in print, online and on air. So how do you create a pitch? Nothing is set in stone, but this is an example of my most successful pitches directed to a journalist on PR subscription sites.

Hi NAME (be courteous and respectful)

SECTION 1: How are you qualified to answer their query (experience counts, so anything that demonstrates your expertise)? Your name and where you are based (e.g. UK). What you do and who you help (keep it attention-grabbing in no more than 12 words).

SECTION 2: Refer to the title of their query (In answer to your query…). How does your commentary help (create a snappy subject title).

SECTION 3.

- Say what your response includes
- Bullet points of what you are including in your response
- Make the content easily memorable
- Use intrigue (e.g. A crisis has your brand in its grip. What are you going to do?)

- Don't miss out on your best bits.

SECTION 4. Ask if they are interested in finding out more and the best way to contact you.

SECTION 5. Share a link to another interview, article, or blog of yours online

Your full name and job title

Your company name

Your website

Your favourite social media channel

When your goals align with a query, consider the outlet and be sure to reference the topic in an engaging way. If you haven't been implementing your value-add message, this is an opportunity to start. If you want to be known as a leading voice in your industry, pitch only to the outlets that help you spread your core message and establish yourself as an expert. If you want to be known as a problem-solver, subscription-based media requests might be a good start for your expertise. You don't need to be an absolute expert; after all, journalists are experts as well, but it's important for you to have a strong understanding of whatever topic you're corresponding about. When pitching to journalists on subscription sites, you should be aware that many of them will remain anonymous. Do not be tempted to send an email to follow up on your HARO pitch. A reporter on HARO rarely invites you to do a deeper dive or asks you to participate in an interview.

The quick guide to pitching directly to a journalist's inbox

When pitching to a journalist, do not assume your first idea is the best. If you come up with an idea within seconds of reading the query, it might have been done before. Be sure not to include any information you cannot back up. When pitching a story, remember that journalists receive hundreds of submissions daily. Many 'compelling' subject lines can end up in a black hole. Be direct, be clear, make the reader pay attention and enable them to easily search for your email later. When pitching a reporter, never assume they will feature your pitch in the article. Choose your words wisely and keep them short and resourceful. Use bullet points where possible. You are pitching a story idea, not writing a book.

The point of the pitch is to get the journalist or producer interested enough to contact you for more details (this is why it is important to include more relevant information for follow-up in your pitch). Their time is valuable, so save it by not making the editor or reporter guess what you have to say. Resist the urge to overwhelm any journalist's inbox; two or three follow-ups are more than enough. They will contact you to let you know if they are interested in what you have to say or will simply quote you. One way to keep track of your commentary is to create a Google Alert in your name.

The best thing I have learned from Michal Smart PR about pitching is how to make journalists' jobs easier and make them want to include my story in their publication or ask for more information. That means you're doing the journalist or editor's job for them or 'DIFT' (Do It for Them) by providing everything they need for the story. That doesn't include creating the story, as that would make them redundant. Just give them everything they need to make a quick decision and do their job. Do remember not to send attachments, as they will rarely be opened.

Cool hack to make PR easier - learn from my mistakes

- Mistake 1: Assuming that I needed to be more significant to contribute. My marketing process is about subject matter expertise or thought leadership marketing, and so many of us need to remember how much knowledge we have inside us. That is why I work with my clients to gain clarity and confidence.
- Mistake 2: Not appreciating the job of journalists and editors and how busy they are, I was offended when there was no response and should have followed up on pitches and press releases.
- Mistake 3: No personalisation. Personalising the pitch is critical and respectful; when emailing somebody, including their name and perhaps something they've written that you've read to begin a mutual relationship.
- Mistake 4: Years ago, when I first started in the media, I used to put the word press release in the email subject, but now I know that the email subject line is essential to open that message. Write it like it's your front page.
- Mistake 5: Thinking that my news is relevant for everyone and forgetting that journalists and editors are interested in their audience and readership rather than a vanity press.

Challenging the status quo and sharing innovation with others is the essence of 'thought leadership'. To become a thought leader, you must have a mindset that knows what needs to be done, a grasp of up-to-date facts that make you a subject matter expert, and a willingness to learn and educate others with integrity as a trusted go-to source of information.

Since I was young, I have questioned and challenged traditional perspectives in the creative industry. I absorb information from various sources and plan imaginative ways to connect that information with a solution-focused mindset. However, when I worked for a charity, I assumed a "Yes" from the press would be because it was charitable work. That wasn't true. Now I'm self-employed and focusing on PR, with a database to reach out to with fresh insights instead of waiting to see what journalists and editors are looking for. However, I still get those helpful PR subscription emails and check Twitter for #journorequests. I don't think I would have been interviewed on national BBC Radio without the experience of pitching on HARO in the early days. Just remember not to pitch in a direct message on social media, as that would be intrusive, and you may get penalised for this.

The case for Thought Leadership as your next PR strategy

Asking thought-provoking questions and going deeper at a conceptual level helps me create reality-ready innovative ideas. The process of opening up new ways of thinking excites me the most, and I would like to leave a legacy that stands for something meaningful. My 5 Key ROI Marketing Principles© is just one example of one of my blueprints and foundations which others can build upon. A memorable and intriguing name for your processes or creating a new terminology for something that has begun trending could be the thing that makes you stand out. That may be the one thing to make the journalist realise you are a thought leader who has considered your industry in a profound way. There is more detail on language in Chapter 13 as your bonus chapter.

The term 'thought leader' is thrown around so often these days that it seems to be losing its meaning. Per the Harvard Business Review, a thought leader "has a valued opinion and stands for something important." Sadly, I see many individuals claiming to be thought leaders, but they're really posting all their thoughts on social media, hoping others will care. To be considered a thought leader, you need to have something valuable to offer. You must have a message that your target audience is receptive to and willing to hear, a message that can help them solve a problem or make their lives better in some way.

A thought leader is someone who can see the bigger picture. They can formulate solutions to problems based on what they have learned and experienced. A thought leader can take an idea and make it tangible. They are able to develop strategies, implement them, and then measure their success. The infectious energy of a thought leader is highly sought after by individuals who value being part of a team. People listen when a thought leader speaks because they know there will be something new or fresh for them. You are recognised for being pioneering and forward-thinking, making you stand out amongst your peers.

The 8 levels of influence in the 'Zone of Authority Circle

Being a pioneer or thought leader is not easy; it requires mental agility and a growth mindset that absorbs and processes knowledge in unique ways to give you a competitive edge. Taking risks, learning from mistakes, making discoveries, and speaking up are all examples of how you can become a pioneer or thought leader in your field. A sound industry knowledge brings self-belief, discipline, action-taking, and positivity people want to be around. The Zone of Authority Circle© is my philosophy for clarifying my personal brand message. The centre part of the zone represents where I aim to be, and it comes with hard work: The Authority Zone.

ZONE OF AUTHORITY CIRCLE

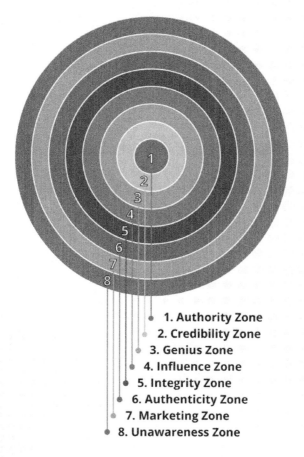

1. Authority Zone
2. Credibility Zone
3. Genius Zone
4. Influence Zone
5. Integrity Zone
6. Authenticity Zone
7. Marketing Zone
8. Unawareness Zone

CREDIBILITY CONFIDENCE: How to Leverage PR as a Start-Up.

Marketing messages have their place, but when we go beyond marketing speak and promotions and delve into what we really know and how much more we can discover, that's when journalists pay attention. I encourage my clients to share their knowledge in a way that creates impact with authenticity and transparency. As much as I support them as thought leaders, I also ensure they don't fall into the trap of trying too hard to be seen as such. As I said before, the value of your opinions comes from them standing for something, not from how much you speak up about them. Real thought leadership attracts a target audience rather than you seeking one out, and generosity brings unsolicited opportunities. Inspiration is a thought leader's key to communicating in a way that engages, enlightens, and encourages others to expand their mind.

Focus on impact instead of profit for transferable skills

While profit is the driving force behind many businesses and self-employed professionals, this is not the case for thought leaders, despite their success. For instance, a true thought leader may be driven by a desire to offer a new perspective on an old problem. By taking an existing idea or product and adding to it in some way, the thought leader provides a valuable service to society. As long as you offer your services at fair market value, it's difficult to find fault with someone who uses their education and experience to provide value to the public.

It's common for those with easily transferable skills to move from business to business and organisation to organisation within their specialisation. This is ideal because it allows thought leaders to continue offering their expertise through various avenues while growing professionally. Whether one is working for themselves or under an employer, growth as a professional and individual depends on thinking outside the box and challenging current notions about how things should be done. As innovators within their fields of expertise, thought leaders lead society by example and by provable results.

What traits do successful thought leaders have in common?

A thought leadership journey begins with recognising your value, finding your voice, creating insight that adds massive value, and featuring in the media and trade publications. Once you realise the best platform for you, you can make a much bigger impression and build a stronger brand. This is the nature of 'thought leadership marketing'. In a crowded market, a thought leadership mindset can help you stand out from the pack. When my clients discover their own credibility as an authority and potential thought leader, their confidence grows, which is very gratifying to see. This is the power of Credibility Confidence. People look to thought leaders to provide them with new ideas and direction. As your contribution to the dialogue pushing your industry forward grows, you can inspire a movement while staying one step ahead of your competition. These are some of the traits to nurture associated with success.

THE TRAITS FOR SUCCESS

Empathy	Patience
Ethics	Passion
Integrity	Connection
Collaboration	Optimism
Humility	Communication
Honesty	Self-Confidence
Loyalty	Determination
Compassion	Resourcefulness
Drive	Insightfulness
Sef-Reliance	Opinion
Enthusiasm	Focus
Curiosity	Charisma
Articulation	Flexibility

CREDIBILITY CONFIDENCE: How to Leverage PR as a Start-Up.

Developing a growth mindset and continuously studying your industry helps you connect new ideas in the field and answer the questions people are asking. This makes you a go-to source for information, which means that people rely on you for answers to their questions. Understanding my niche market has given me fluency when I engage with them, and their terminologies become a language that I willingly share with them. As a start-up with a 10-year history as a Media Officer at a charity, my ability to communicate ranges from easy-read format to academic papers; communications are definitely my thing. Knowing this helps me to appreciate my ability to explain complex concepts in accessible and inclusive language. How does your past shape your expertise?

Four tactics you can use today to start pitching your thought leadership

1. **Establish your visionary message by connecting ideas from various sources**

   Massive innovations are rare, but how ideas are visualised and remembered can make them unique. As a conceptual designer with a background in the visual arts, visionary perspectives are paramount. Some of my clients have said they do not recognise themselves in the bio I create for them when pitching to the media. As the information is indeed accurate, it is only my outside perspective that makes the difference. For me, knowledge is power and has always been a valuable commodity. Its communication is a currency. Everyone's frame of reference is unique as they see the world through their own lens and from a different angle. I have supported business owners to visualise industry knowledge on subjects such as e-commerce, sleep consultancy, beauty products, client-acquisition software, mindset and journaling, cyber security, and entrepreneurship to create insightful visual presentations from their own viewpoints. One of my coaching clients invented the word 'Sofala' for her latest online group meetings. This acronym for structure, organisation, focus, accountability, and action has become part of her unique and memorable message.

2. **Communicate your message with clarity and genuinely listen to others.**

We can communicate in so many ways. Copywriting is an ideal channel to spotlight truly remarkable communications. However, public speaking is essential in everything we do, from our body language to marketing content creation. It comes more naturally now to me as a previous member of Toastmasters and the Woman Who Academy. Toastmasters International is a non-profit organisation that helps people gain confidence and improve their public speaking skills. The Woman Who Academy inspires women in business to recognise their achievements and become local role models for others. I talk more about the variety of communication needs in Chapter 10.

Continually improving interpersonal skills will up-level your relationships and clearly and concisely market your message. Transferring ideas from your mind's eye to others effectively is a competency vital to transactions in business. I have noticed that becoming an active listener enables me to understand and increases my ability to react to my audience's needs. Listening is not a passive activity; it requires commitment and involvement. I listen to the point of immersion in my client's thought processes and find my way out through interpretation. If you listen honestly, you will be perceived as curious, considerate, and more thoughtful. This, in turn, builds trust.

3. Cultivate your modesty mindset to build credibility with a gratitude mentality

The more I learn, the more I realise that I have only scratched the surface of the world's wealth of knowledge. Access to the information highway is a gift that, as thought leaders, we can be grateful for. The ability to process data, channel it into new thinking and inspire others is a privilege. Acknowledging this fact keeps me humble.

Regular media features require new perspectives, creating a further need for you to continue personal development and inspiration. Through thought leadership, PR is a relationship-building exercise, making it more comfortable when your audience rather than a sales pitch. People are shrewd and sceptical, so when they see you feature as a subject-matter expert in the media, it is considered an independent third-party endorsement and not self-governed. Advancement of a thought leader will develop naturally based on the effectiveness of their message and mentoring rather than the forced attribute of advertising.

4. Reinforce your message consistently to become a recognised leader with integrity.

As you know, integrity is at the top of my Source Trust Triangle. It leads down to the benefit of your knowledge, qualifications, and reliability, eventually leading to trust and becoming a source of wisdom. Awareness of this process enables me to isolate the effectiveness of each element and where I need to enhance my expertise. In marketing, as a thought leader, I aim to be an invited commentator in people's everyday lives. One that they come to rely on by habit in their newsfeed or emails and one that people want to follow.

Without the following, any form of leadership becomes impossible.

I put PR at the helm of my marketing strategy, focusing on 'earned media'. This helps me stay focused on what is important and newsworthy, such as timeliness and the future impact of your message within your industry.

CHAPTER 4

The Power of Newsworthy Content

The Art of Creating Stories with Impact

When you hear the word 'news', what do you think of it? Facts? Statistics? Stories about politics and war and the economy? Okay, you might have a point there. Let's be honest; the news is not always the most exciting thing in the world to read. That doesn't mean we can't make it more engaging! People want something they can relate to in their news. Something that will grab their attention and keep them reading. Newsworthiness is a concept every start-up needs to understand and keep in mind as they write and edit stories. It refers to how relevant, interesting, or important news stories are to their audience. Readers want to learn about things that will impact them in some way, but they don't want to hear about your business if it doesn't have any bearing on their lives. If your story falls into one of the following categories, you've got a winner. The following tips I have used to pitch directly to the media successfully.

Your next big story. What is considered newsworthy?

WHAT IS CONSIDERED NEWSWORTHY?

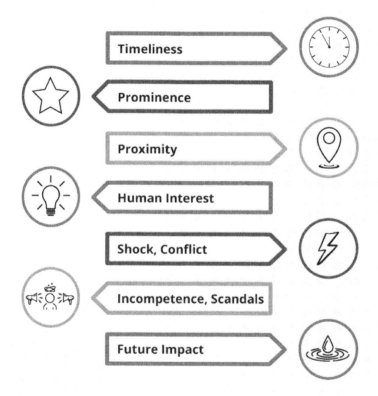

The impact of the story is important to the lives of your readers. It tells them why a story is important and explains the consequences of that news. Timeliness addresses the question, "Why are you telling me this now?" Prominence poses the question: "Who is associated with the impact of this story?" People want to know about celebrities, politicians, and business leaders because they look up to and aspire to be like them. As a start-up, it's worth noting that we are earning the right to be quoted or cited. We have to prove our authority and gain prominence. Proximity is all about understanding how a story impacts your chosen audience and if there's anything unexpected about it. The story's proximity impacts whether it's a story that matters to the reader. If it happened far away or didn't directly affect anyone in your audience, it won't be interesting to them.

People are also drawn to conflict, which is why they love good news, often balanced by bad news. Most people like two-sided arguments, especially those with a hero and a villain. Therefore, news stories that are shocking and scandalous have all the hallmarks of being newsworthy. In contrast, human-interest stories, those feel-good tales of triumph over adversity or uplifting stories about someone who does something nice for a stranger, are among the most shared news stories and are often considered to be the easiest to sell. But they can be overused and often need to catch up on being genuinely newsworthy.

'Currency' is a term used to describe an idea whose time has come. However, some stories will still end up getting passed over regardless due to media priorities. Of all the newsworthy categories mentioned, I feel that future impact is where start-ups can make their mark. How are you changing the world with your business? What change-making insights do you have? Timeliness is key here: if the story is no longer relevant or new, it's old news. If your story involves one of these types of elements, you may have written a front-pager!

If it is the story of the year, it still needs to be told right

Getting caught up in the thrill of being asked to be interviewed by a journalist is very easy. After all, media attention is exciting and can generate new business opportunities and a reputation as an expert in your field. But there are some things you should keep in mind when dealing with the media. To create stories that matter, your content needs to come from a credible source of newsworthy information, as described in The Source Trust Triangle, with integrity, benefits, qualification, reliability, and trust.

Sometimes our news as a start-up differs from what makes the story newsworthy; we could have overlooked something that provokes deeper thought. Remember the story of my client with the relationship matchmaking business. She needed to discuss how we had forgotten about body language through the COVID-19 lockdown as we were communicating online and the unrealistic expectations many people had about finding relationships with television dating programmes. It was only after being relevant that she then mentioned her business. The heading of her pitch was "Local Agony Aunt Helps Singletons To Stop Visiting Dating Sites and Start Meeting Real People", with an email subject line of Fun New SINGLES Events/ LAUNCHING New Dating & Matchmaking Service. The pitch was a success!

Non-spammy yet attention-grabbing emails light up a journalist's inbox

An email subject line can mean the difference between a news story being read and one being deleted. To make sure your email is opened, you need to pay special attention to your subject line. Here are some tips for writing attention-grabbing headlines that will ensure people actually see what you have to say.

- **Do keep it short**

  Only so many characters can be seen in a subject line as may be seen on a mobile phone. If you put too much detail into the subject line, it may be cut off by the sender's outbox or the reader's phone. On mobiles, you can only read 25-30 characters

- **Do keep it snappy**

  The subject line is the first thing people see, so it needs to grab their attention immediately. Don't use the words press releases or "PR" as your subject line; if you want to use them, do so in the body of your pitch instead.

- **Do not write spam**

  A salesy, marketing email subject could land you in the journalist's spam folder. The subject can be the last thing you write. It should be engaging but also contain a hook to get journalists to open it. Journalists love data and visuals. Include them in the subject "Video shows...", "See how..." or "Watch..."

- **Do connect to the body of your pitch**

  While you want a short headline that doesn't give away all of your story details, it should feel relevant to your pitch.

- **Do use characters**

  You may find that inserting different characters may help to break up the content of your subject line in an interesting way. Do send the email to yourself a few times to see how you notice your email subject line within your inbox. (For example, I use: || or / or :)

Here are some of my pitch subjects that were opened:

- Are They Qualified? 77,945 Salespeople in Manufacturing and Counting
- MEL B: Real Life || 13 Abuse Survivors & New Book [HOPE For Victims To Escape]
- Empowering Women Survivors BEDFORD Event: TEDx Speaker/ June Conference
- ADAPTABILITY: Article < Charity Worker/ Public Speaker's Perspective >
- PRESS PLUGS: UK Business B2C Bringing The Red Carpet Glamour To Customers
- MIDLANDS: NEW Partnership / Version 2 CRM Launch Game Changer for SMEs

Know your audience by getting personal with journalists

When you pitch to the media, it's their readers that matter to them, not you, and not your start-up aspirations. You are privileged to provide a service as a subject matter expert, and they want readers and shares or 'syndication'. Syndicating content is the practice of online news sites, magazines and blogs republishing their own stories on a range of different sites.

If you don't give them what they want, they will go to someone who can. If you just tell them what you think they need to know about your product or service, it won't work.

Be sure to work for it and show the journalist how much you value this opportunity to make an impact. Provide the media outlet with everything they need. Journalists are busy people and don't want to go hunting for information, so make it really easy for them by providing a one-stop-shop kit where they can access everything they might need in a folder, including press releases, high-resolution photographs, liftable quotes, answers to questions they may ask and any other material that may help them. I will usually write the press release, add it to a shared folder on Google with high-resolution images and share the URL link in the body of my pitch. They will appreciate your professionalism, and it will help them remember you when there is something else that might interest them in the future.

Personalising your pitch can make all the difference for a journalist. Whether you're pitching an event, a blog post, or a story, if you have time, try to tailor your pitch to that individual journalist. Make it specific to your journalist – do you know a mutual friend? Is there something topical in the news that might make your story more relevant? Are you a local company? Remember, don't blanket send. If you're going to send out one email, then go for it. But if you send out 20 or 30, then don't be surprised when journalists start ignoring you. It's a waste of time on both sides as journalists will have less time to spend on each pitch and probably feel like they're dealing with an automated service.

Get the right journalist for the topic. The best way is to check out the publication's website to see who writes on similar topics (if there are any). Then look at their Twitter feed to see what interests them and where they've been mentioned recently. Once you've found the right person to approach, try searching for their name in Google news to see what topics they've recently covered. I have found that a great time to pitch is Tuesday to Thursday between 11 am and 2 pm. Mondays are busy for all of us, including journalists catching up on the past weekend's events. On Fridays, we all like to wind down. If you want your story published quickly, early morning is best. Remember, journalists get inundated with emails at night and late afternoon.

When you are a trusted source for the media, then you will be transported into the when to open, not if to open. Be ahead of the game by doing your research and anticipating what will become newsworthy. Be sincere; sources are sceptical of anyone trying to use them. Don't just send press releases and run; offer to speak with journalists when they have questions or a story idea. You're already halfway there if you can provide expertise on a relevant topic to your business.

How to create a press release when you are not an expert

A well-written press release is handy for two reasons. First, it gives journalists a good idea of what to expect from your story. Second, it is an extension of your brand, so journalists can write about your company without contacting you first. To achieve these aims, you need to include certain elements in each press release. I can't stress enough that journalists are extremely busy people – they're not going to spend time reading a long document if you can't give them a good reason why they should do so. If a journalist receives your press release in their email inbox and sees it's more than one page long, they probably won't bother reading past the first few lines at the top of the first page because they know they don't have time. That's why it's crucial that you write concisely. The worst thing you can do is write a massive wall of text or publish a press release that is not public domain. This is a huge turn-off for journalists and an easy way for you to lose credibility with potential customers before you've even had a chance to sell them anything.

ANATOMY OF A PRESS RELEASE

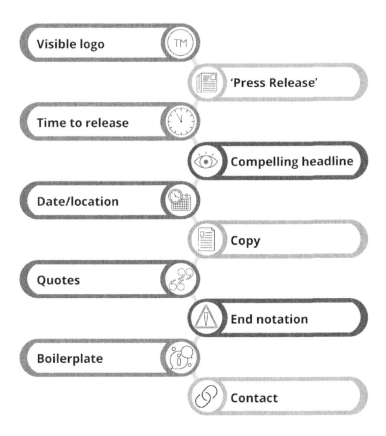

- Visible logo — TM
- 'Press Release'
- Time to release
- Compelling headline
- Date/location
- Copy
- Quotes
- End notation
- Boilerplate
- Contact

CREDIBILITY CONFIDENCE: How to Leverage PR as a Start-Up.

My press releases use just four sections. The first is a concise description of the story. If it's read in isolation, it should hook the reader and summarise the content. The second section contains more information and detail. Then the third can be a quote from someone involved in the story. If you have quotes from others involved in the story, include them in the press release, but only if they're relatively short. I may also divide these sections, so they are easier on the eye. Only include longer quotes if you're certain they'll be relevant to an editor's interests (for instance, if it's a celebrity). Otherwise, keep them out of your press release; or it might get lost in their inboxes before it gets read. After the last paragraph, I then add ## Ends and underneath the words 'Notes to editors' before the fourth and last section, called the 'boilerplate'. The boilerplate describes your company and key business information at the bottom of a press release. In addition to giving interested journalists information about your business, it adds credibility to your press release. It also gives you a place to add a call to action and a link to your website.

Though they're often confused, a press release and a pitch are not the same things. The press release is the message, and the email pitch persuades the journalist that their readers will be interested in this message. There is some overlap as some elements can be present in both the press release and the media pitch. Confusion between them arises because to be successful, a press release and its accompanying pitch should both have the same goal - to interest media outlets in your story so they'll want to share it with their readers or viewers. Knowing what makes a good pitch can turn an otherwise mundane story into something special and newsworthy.

2-3 paragraph pitches are super simple and highly effective

My best pitches include a catchy heading and are only 2 to 3 paragraphs long. That's it. We're not even talking about the body of your content, just the pitch. If you have an idea for a news story, article, blog post, photo essay, or whatever, you should be able to say what it is in 2 or 3 sentences. I know we've all been taught that 'more is better' and 'short is for chumps', but trust me, in a fast-paced world, brevity works. When people think about something for less time, they are more likely to actually do something about it instead of forgetting about it five seconds later.

When you're pitching a story to a media outlet, it's important to establish the parameters of your request. Is the story exclusive? If so, this restricts where it can be published and shared. I don't recommend exclusivity. I have only provided one article for an online magazine that was 'exclusive', which I now regret. Is the story for immediate release? This tells them how quickly they have to act on the information you're sharing. They may need to get the article up before you have time to develop your piece or before other outlets have had a chance to get their own stories out. Remember, you should include an explanation of who you are and why you're reaching out.

Don't be too stalkerish in building rapport with a journalist; they've probably received tons of requests like yours, so don't make them feel like another person trying to sell something or promote their interests. Finally, you can include a note at the end of your email asking them not to copy and paste your email to share it with anyone else; this has been known to trigger spam filters and cause your email to go unread by the recipient.

Why the press release is still relevant

If you are creating a media plan, the press release is still an important part of your strategy. The press release has been around for over a hundred years and may never go out of style. There are many reasons why it is still used today: The press release is a concise announcement containing information regarding an exciting event or announcement that will be of interest to journalists. It is distributed to various people, from editors and producers in broadcast media to newspaper reporters. The information in the news release is designed to pique the reader's interest and lead them to want more information about the subject at hand. The goal of a press release is to get covered by one or more media outlets, leading to increased brand awareness and potential consumers for your product or service.

It's no secret that journalists get pitched all the time. If you want to break through the noise, you need to do more than just email them. Build relationships and engage on their social media. Find them on social media and have a strategy you can use for at least six months, then start over again. Spend 20 minutes daily engaging with journalists; most use fast-paced social media such as Twitter or follow them on LinkedIn. Check out their feed to see what they are talking about. When pitching, a rule of thumb for me is to pitch and follow up a week later if the news isn't time bound or two days later if it is urgent.

Hey [name of the journalist], thank you for sharing this story

Keep in touch with the journalist so they know you are still around and willing to help when they want some info or want to talk about something. When you have been featured in the media, sharing the news all over your socials and thanking them is good practice. When you get featured on a website, magazine, or newspaper, they will likely share your article on their social media accounts. This is another way people find out about your article and brand. This is why it is important to thank them for posting about you because it increases the likelihood of them sharing again in the future.

Create a pitch that journalists want to reply to

Some pitches are newsworthy for different reasons. Magazines are often looking to feature brands that impress them too. Here is an example of one of my successful magazine pitches:

Hi [Name]

As seen in John Lewis and Women's Health, the UK's upcoming inclusive skincare brand DeRoiste Natural Beauty would like to be included in [magazine name]

Founder Esther Roche has been named one of the UK's most inspirational and dynamic female entrepreneurs by the f:Entrepreneur '#ialso100' campaign. Her mission is to inspire and encourage others to embrace the skin they were born with and not compromise their skin health due to societal pressure. Examples of media coverage: [links to] Business Mondays and Bedford Today

Mum of 5, Esther spent two and half years researching the power of plant-based ingredients. Indeed, she was also recognised for being the "One to Watch" at the Woman Who Achieves Awards and received a business boost from Retail Entrepreneur Theo Paphitis following her winning tweet during the 'Small Business Sunday'.

Esther created her skincare products with her family's sensitive skin in mind.

DeRoiste products are:

- Gender-inclusive, vegan, organic
- Suitable for all skin tones
- Natural, organic, no fragrances, cruelty-free and made in the UK
- 100 % natural ingredients include Vitamin C, pomegranate, turmeric, hyaluronic acid, green tea, kojic acid, liquorice, and rosehip

If you would like to find out more, please email me or call [number].

For further information, please do check out Esther's website www.deroistenaturalbeauty.com.

Sincerely

Abbi Head

PR & Communications Strategist

LinkedIn: https://www.linkedin.com/in/abbi-littleprrockmarketing/

Email: abbi@littleprrockmarketing.co.uk

www.littleprrockmarketing.co.uk

CHAPTER 5

Essential PR Tactics Made Easy:

Start The Conversation and Get More Recognition

The more often you are seen in the media, the more credible and familiar you look to potential customers and referral sources. Even if they haven't read a full article or seen an entire clip where you were featured, they will have seen your picture enough times to recognise your face and this familiarity breeds trust.

It is worth keeping an eye on what journalists include in their social media. We call their interests the 'beat,' or specific topic they cover. The routes journalists take and the people they talk to while doing their job serve as a good example of how they gather information. Checking out their social media feed is a great way to start a conversation with them, as you can comment on their post or send them a personal message thanking them for sharing your work. This type of relationship-building is helpful because once they know more about what you do, they might remember when they need someone to talk to about that topic. You can also build relationships with journalists interested in covering issues related to what you wrote about in previous media stories.

In addition, you can build your credibility by discussing your core expertise in developing relationships with other experts. Repurposing your expertise is an excellent way to expand your network and provide value to others outside your immediate sphere of influence. For example, you could interview another expert on one of the topics you are known for in the media, put that information and your own into a blog post or report, and share that information through various channels such as social media, emails and so on.

By consistently creating media attention, you can position yourself as a thought leader and an expert in your field. This content will help boost your visibility and credibility, attract potential clients, and help to generate leads. You can continue to develop new content assets by creating books, white papers, and blog posts. (The government uses white papers to outline their proposals for future legislation.) Depending on your business you can also answer questions that clients or prospects often ask, enhancing your credibility with those who know you best, people who have purchased from you before or those who are familiar with your brand. However, if you have knowledge that becomes your 'secret sauce', do protect it as proprietary information.

The 'Stacking Strategy' and repurposed content

So, what do I mean by 'Stacking' your media coverage? Every time you reach out to the media and are featured, you create a building block of Credibility Confidence that you can stack on top of the last. The best way to reach your goals, big or small, is to break them into smaller, more manageable steps and monitor your progress.

Quantify your accomplishments and keep track of your progress in real time so that you can stay on course and build confidence as you see your accomplishments pile up. Repurposed content is a great way to show journalists, customers, and stakeholders that you're trustworthy. By using curated repurposed content, you can show a journalist has recognised your work, which is both flattering and helpful in gaining attention and marketing. You can use the 'Stacking Strategy©' to gain media coverage and then share the content in several ways, including the following:

- Create an AS SEEN IN graphic for your email footer
- Use it in your business plan when pitching to investors
- Create a Google post or advertisement
- Create a website banner and display it on your homepage
- Share in social media weekly in different formats:
  - Create graphics with quotes
  - Use the content in a social media post text
  - Talk about the topic and share the link with a video
- Create a blog or news post on your website about the same content and URL link or download
- Share with stakeholders in annual meetings and reports
- Put the URL link on your Linktree (or similar)
- Add the QR code to marketing material
- Use in your branded presentations
- Design a landing page and expand on the contents of the feature
- Write a keynote speech about it and share it in your networking
- Print it, frame it, and hang it somewhere noticeable where customers will see it
- Use it to share in another pitch to a journalist, editor, or influencer
- Use it as evidence to create a branded proof point as you do with testimonials
- Include it in award entries
- Add the feature to your media kit
- Purchase a "tear sheet" (torn from a magazine) to validate what you have to offer
  - Design a handout at tradeshows or networking events
  - Leave behind when you do local speaking gigs
  - Leave it as reading material in your office
- Introduce yourself to further media publications
- Mention it in a book like this one

Credibility Confidence: your actions and decisions define your character

Ask yourself what is the best version of you, the one you aspire to be, what you would be doing, and do it. Even when it's really hard and it's the last thing you want to do, you'll be glad you did it. Most confident people live by a value system and make their decisions based on it, even when it's hard and not necessarily in their best interest in the short-term but in the interest of the greater good.

Fear of failure can freeze even the most ambitious person. But remember that failure is not the enemy. If you set big goals and have big dreams, you're going to feel overwhelmed and inevitably feel like you can't do it. In those moments, look inside yourself, gather every ounce of courage, and just keep going. Every wildly successful person has been afraid before they accomplish their goals. Still, they kept working anyway because what they were trying to accomplish was more important and urgent than their fear of failure.

Think about how much you want to reach your goal, then put your fear aside and just keep going for one more day at a time. Aim toward Credibility Confidence and foster it daily. It can be elusive, so when we do acknowledge our own self-worth and feel assured in our convictions, it makes us more determined than ever to forge ahead. This creates a cycle of positive momentum where we not only believe in ourselves with an open mind, but we also plan our future with the liberation of thought. It affects our attitude to everything we do, the decisions we make and how we approach the challenges in our life. Without confidence, it is harder to stay focused because negative self-talk destroys our good intentions, and even if that does not beat us, it makes making choices more difficult.

Inner confidence is a combination of being assured while embracing our own strengths and weaknesses. Too much confidence, however, can come at a cost. It is so easy to become complacent when we feel confident, and we can make mistakes when we go into overdrive.

Confidence may come naturally with experience, or sometimes we deliberately take time out to look at our achievements to boost our self-esteem. It is important to congratulate ourselves for our accomplishments because it releases us from our inhibitions to praise ourselves and use that energy to drive ourselves forward. It becomes part of our internal dialogue. It is the words of encouragement we heard as a child, the compliments we receive daily, the little wins and the sense of pride we feel in recognising ourselves for who we really are. Therefore, confidence can be nurtured or restricted every day.

Making decisions quicker comes with confidence, knowing that we can rely on ourselves independently and trust in what we know. Underneath, we can be paddling frantically, yet our confidence propels us forward and hides our anxieties from others. It will find solutions first and face issues practically. It is the part of us that believes our version of our situation and seamlessly filters our options enabling us to take bold steps. It also hides when we are alone, fearful, or tired. When we let our guard drop, it is essential to find reminders of what makes us feel valued, appreciated, and rewarded so that we can bounce back to being confident again.

Start communicating Credibility Confidence with your customers today!

In our own hearts and minds, we can grow in confidence. Everyone's journey is different; our experiences shape us, so comparing ourselves to others will lead us toward negative emotions. Without regaining confidence, we will become rooted in that place of self-doubt. It embraces the opportunities placed before us as we progress with our lives, both personally and professionally.

Confidence helps us to conquer uncertainty in ourselves, master our emotions, and communicate honestly and effectively. It is expressed in our assertiveness and knowing that we are enough. It is both a goal and a resting place. Once it is obtained, it is important to keep the encouraging feelings simmering. We can share our confidence with others to inspire and motivate them. It is a sense of equality. It is within you. It is within me. It is the best version of ourselves and gives us the power to stand fearlessly and present who we are to the world. That has a value or ROI in itself.

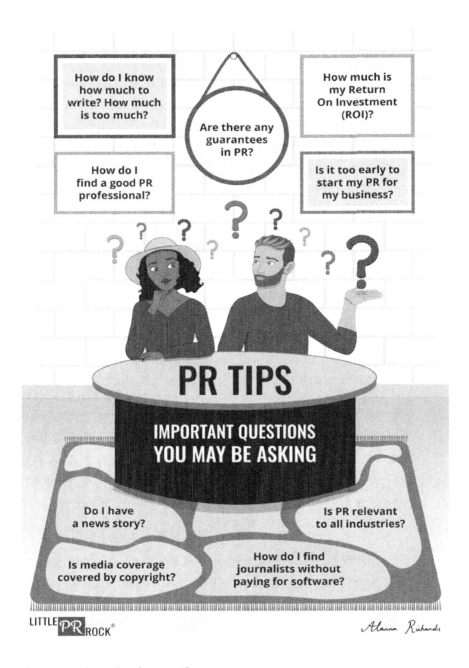

Frequently asked questions:

Some of the questions I was asked about PR when writing this book include:

1. Is it too early to start my PR for my business?

I started out with PR and thought leadership marketing as my business strategy from the onset. The investment has been worth it because it started a course where I am financially valued now more than when I started my business. It also gives me the reassurance that I have worked hard to make an impact and, therefore, am worth it. The responsibility keeps me motivated to achieve more. Although I have experience in PR, pitching your own business takes work. I have answered requests over the years that have helped me to go from a novice at pitching myself to the Credibility Confidence to pitch national and global media. I now feel more able to reach out to a journalist directly without receiving their requests by just following their beat and adding value.

2. Do I have a news story?

We all have something to share; it just depends on what you are comfortable with people knowing about you. I always say, don't share your entire life story in your first press release just to get media coverage. Think about the times in your life when you learned valuable lessons and why they are relevant to what you have to say.

For example, my mother worked at a school for many years. She was responsible for delivering refreshments at sports events, waitressing at meals for their governors, or during events such as glamorous balls. I helped her sometimes, and the school had a family feel that I remember fondly. The thing that sticks in my mind as a PR professional is that she was enthusiastic about the school and spoke to all the guests and visitors about its history, the buildings' architecture, the school's academic statistics, and anything she felt passionate about. At the time, she was demonstrating her PR skills. I have inherited her communications ability and now find my place in the PR industry, reaching out to businesses to unlock the PR potential in their workforce too. Telling you that small snippet of my life brings a human aspect to my story. I can then continue with my expertise, knowing that it has relevance even today as businesses struggle with the impacts of social media and having their employees as potential spokespeople.

3. Is PR relevant to all industries?

I think that it is, because where there are humans, there are stories. Think about what makes a great story and the experts who are interviewed. When you start out, it is easy to think you must create PR stunts to get coverage. You need to research the news and magazines, listen to the radio, or watch television programmes that relate to or are relevant to what you do. That way, you will be up-to-date and newsworthy. If you take some time to consider what you already know in detail, you will find something relevant, timely, impactful, and of media interest. The research will keep you informed about your industry and can improve the way you do business. It may also help you make decisions about your business planning in the future.

4. How do I know how much to write? How much is too much?

Journalists get hundreds of emails daily, so you only need the essentials. A good way to keep yourself on track is to write a stream of thoughts and then make notes on the side as you read it back. What was the text that stuck with you? What did you want to know more about? What seemed irrelevant?

Then you can section the notes out to make separate stories. Many organisational tools can help you to plan your content and create a PR strategy. That strategy may lead to a book like mine has for me. We have covered pitching. However, I find the press release process I use in Chapter 4 keeps me on track, and a specific word count is generally provided for guest articles and blogs.

5. Does copyright cover media coverage?

The Newspaper Licensing Agency (NLA) lists all publications that hold the copyright to your media coverage when you publish with them. (Please note, these include local newspapers). You own your press release content, but you do not once it has been edited for publication. There are fines for a breach of copyright, including screenshotting the website page or using the headline or teaser images in social posts. You can purchase a licence for ten news articles or more at various prices. Be careful using the logos of organisations, too, especially in a way that looks like they have endorsed you. The BBC has an application form for using its logo, which is copyrighted, including all television and radio versions. It is also important to be mindful when you say, "As Seen In" and "As Featured In", which are very different usages.

Some tips to help you overcome copyright issues include:

- Ask permission from the media (not the journalist)
- Share the QR code to the story
- Take a section of the key message and reword it for use
- Share the original photos with a rewritten quote

- Share the story about how you got featured in the publication
- Create an Alt Text version of your article images: Alt Text is an accessibility feature that provides a visual description of photos for people with visual impairments.
- Copy the URL and use this as a hyperlink
- Use the terms: "Contributor to"

6. How do I find journalists without paying for software?

One of the easiest ways to find journalists is to read articles they have written, which will tell you what they write about and their full names. If you want to craft a relevant pitch, you need to find out what's relevant to that contact. You may simply be able to Google them. Some newspapers will have full email addresses on their website; others will have generic email. I follow journalists on social media in order to build relationships. Remember, do not pitch to them on social media, though. A media database is just a list of names and email addresses. And while your purchased databases might give a bit of background for each journalist, this data could be out of date. Journalists change interests, take on new gigs, and move to different outlets, so PR professionals get caught out too.

7. How much is my Return On Investment (ROI)?

This is always the question that PR struggles to measure. PR is an investment, and I do not evaluate the results by the number of acquired customers. It is easier to assess ROI now that we have digital PR and social media. For example, I mentioned on LinkedIn that I had landed a client in an online magazine and immediately received a direct message asking if I could do the same for them. You need to take a risk when you start out and link your PR to your marketing to get an ROI. As I said, PR is about the long game. The aim is to become the subject-matter expert whose reputation precedes them. The one that people turn to for advice. That will boost your confidence and self-esteem and help you to take your business to the next level. There are some tips on using your Credibility Confidence in your sales process in Chapter 10.

My ROI is measured within the following areas. Benchmarking results are explained further in Chapter 11:

- Respect: A bedrock of intellectual property (IP)
- Recognition: Regular third-party independent endorsement
- Resilience: Engagement strategy with quality, not quantity social posts
- Reputation: Representation from professional communication
- Reinforcement: Your USP visualised with content for repurposing

8. Are there any guarantees in PR?

No. But some unethical people do try to take advantage of the system. Their efforts could also be discovered and deleted, making it a bad investment. The press for example, operates under a code of conduct that prohibits editorial coverage in exchange for money or other favours. For these journalists to accept money in exchange for coverage would be career suicide. You may quibble with the quality or fairness of an individual article, but in my view, it is not worth it.

As I mentioned earlier, many online information hubs and publications can help you to boost your visibility legally. I have written articles and interviews for many media outlets with no financial cost. They are also open about paid options in the publication process, such as the ability to be published quicker, edit your article once online, include backlinks or submit your article in the first instance. Backlinks connect one web page to another, with certain words or phrases (known as anchor text) highlighted. This generates traffic from a qualified audience and boosts rankings for the brand's website on search engine pages. This backlink strategy is popular among bloggers and website owners who want to increase the popularity of their own websites.

One way to guarantee that you will be considered is to work with integrity and get your timing right. As a PR award winner, I am only now just confident enough to apply to contribute to Forbes. That will most likely be from an introduction by another contributor, not by paying someone to feature my story.

9. **How do I find a good PR professional?**

PR is like every other industry, and reputation for someone like me is crucial. As you start out, you may have some funds, but be aware that PR agencies can be very costly when you can do some of the work yourself for free. As a start-up, you have time to plan your PR strategy and learn how to manage it; this is essential so that you know what is involved when a PR professional takes over. My best advice is to take things one step at a time and learn from every step whilst avoiding too many catastrophic mistakes. A PR and Communications Strategist like me may help you with workshops that can bring together everything you need to get started in a media or press kit. You are looking for someone who cares about you and your business, not just about getting the news story published. That is why I believe earning media coverage is important and does not provide guarantees.

If you are looking for a workshop to get yourself or your business media-ready, then email me at: abbi@littleprrockmarketing.co.uk.

CHAPTER 6

Success Is the Product of Failure

Turning Rejection into Results

In the world of PR, rejection comes in many forms. I have learned some valuable lessons from pitching to journalists in the press, television, radio and print or online magazines. When a journalist seemed enthusiastic about my pitch, I would tell my clients that they were excited. Then they got excited too.

There was one pitch that I sent, and the journalist's reply was, "Love this, thanks, will pitch something on how to make your room sparkle. Keep you posted." I told my client, who was obviously thrilled, and we waited patiently for several days. When I returned home from a speakers' weekend boot camp, I checked my mail, and there was no response. I followed up on the pitch, but again, no answer. Finally, after several days I received an email saying, "Sorry, it's been a hectic week. I'm afraid this hasn't been picked up, but if anything changes, I will let you know. Have a lovely weekend."

Nothing changed, so my weekend was not lovely because I knew I had to tell my client on Monday that we had been unsuccessful this time. At times like this, I recognise my communications role between my client and what they want to promote and the journalist looking for something newsworthy. When you do your own PR as a start-up, you need to take on this position yourself so the lessons may be more emotive.

Your digital footprint is great PR. Do not destroy it.

Not long after I pitched again to another journalist, and this time the message was more direct. "Thanks for getting in touch; I'll pitch the editor. Do you have any more images to send across?" read the email message. This was the last time I got excited at this stage of pitching because it was again unsuccessful. There was a glimmer of hope because this journalist needed something in a particular niche. I had a client in that niche, so I followed up a second time with another story angle. Bingo! A reply. Not what I was expecting at the time, as I had written about the rise of my client, who was achieving extraordinary business success. The email from the journalist asked about a specific part of that client's epic journey; they said, "Can she talk about finances and income support etc." It was a lesson I haven't forgotten because I protect my clients rather like a buffer.

I see so many stories about business owners where their whole life is included 'chapter and verse'. There is nothing left in their life story that hasn't been said. So, what's next? I suggest only telling the part of the story relevant to what you need to say because it is then your credibility story. I have researched past clients and been flummoxed by what I have found on the first page of Google. I believe there is no reason to sell your soul for media coverage. It can be tempting to provide shock value just to get in the press. I don't believe all publicity is good publicity because I work with clients who are building their online reputation for the long haul. I have seen the results of that shocking story being hard to ignore on someone's digital footprint. I would not recommend creating a PR stunt just to get noticed. I would rather be rejected.

As a start-up, you have a blank canvas to begin the painting of your business story. I have learned that features in the broadsheets are difficult to override from page one of Google, so remember, whatever you share may last a lifetime. Protect yourself with your digital footprint and legacy of media coverage from day one.

Recently I received a message from a fellow new business owner saying: "I would love a chat when we see each other again, Abbi. I've hit a brick wall with PR. The only stories that get picked up are my weird personal ones, and I don't want potential partners, grant funding assessors and investors to Google me and read about my belly button phobia!"

The second thing is to be timely with information in your industry and stay on top of trends. I asked a client to trust me once to get a story during the COVID-19 pandemic about how it had affected her industry. The client challenged the final press release, so I amended it, and the story was rejected. As a start-up, trust your gut; this goes back to being a thought leader. There is no room for sweeping statements without evidence for me in PR today; even though you are experiencing your industry personally, back it up with facts.

Behave like Teflon: keep going in a category of your own

The day I received my letter from the IPO Office refusing to trademark my initial business name was a turning point in my understanding of intellectual property, my reputation, and public relations. When I started out, my business name was 'The Visuals Adviser,' and I was making an impact in my local networking circles. I was on a global news channel to talk about my creative business planning course, and I was proud, but I had also made a mistake. Whether trademarking a name, a process or giving value to a journalist, novelty and originality are the most important things. I was rejected, but my reputation had been established with the name 'The Visuals Adviser'. However, to receive maximum credibility, I wanted a trademark symbol and the security of knowing that my business name was unique.

When you get responses like this, it can be disheartening. So be the Teflon go-to person and persevere. Though you may assume you've been unsuccessful, opportunities are around the corner. I sent a pitch to the wrong email address; when I checked via Twitter, it turned out that the producer had changed his email address, but I didn't give up! I sent another email to the producer. Unfortunately, it was too late for the original pitch as the story had already aired. This second pitch provided an opportunity to mention one of my other clients live on national radio.

After thinking about the pitch that never made it into a producer's inbox, I reflected on something I once heard: If you're genuinely sending out pitches that are helpful, credible, and relevant, then journalists are less likely to unsubscribe or throw you into their spam folder. Relevance is a factor in determining whether journalists will respond to your pitches or not. Timing, however, is the most important factor. For example, I once pitched to a journalist to write about my passion for designing jewellery in an article about PR professionals' hobbies. Due to my workload, I sent my pitch last minute. Despite not being included, the journalist made special efforts to reply. He said that on this occasion, it was first come, first serve.

There are many requests with a sense of urgency. They need to be answered in hours, so I suggest that you have several ready-to-go pitches at hand for these occasions. Practising your pitching is essential to get you ready for success, but remember that the follow-up is just as important and needs to provide consistency. Persistence enabled one of my clients to be featured in My Weekly when a journalist downloaded her product. Having "As Seen In My Weekly" is something that in itself is beneficial, regardless of sales.

One of the most difficult rejections I faced was for a client who had a product they wanted to feature in celebrity gift bags which were a highlight at a big music event. The response to my pitch was, "Sounds perfect". They asked my client to send a sample of the gift offered inside a sample bag. We were unprepared and sent two sample pots and a voucher designed in a hurry. The news wasn't good because once the items had been sent to the radio station, there was no news. It was Crickets again. The moral of that tale is to be professionally prepared to send quality items at short notice. There is always another opportunity as events such as these are annual.

The truth about adverts, advertorials, and sponsored content

Sometimes an advertorial (half editorial and half advert) is the best way to get the balance of advert and editorial just right. However, there are downsides to writing paid articles. First, you may feel it is less worthy than 'earned media'. You can pitch to a sponsored journalist, and then they suggest payment options. It doesn't feel like a win. However, I think it is essential to occasionally pay for your content to be visible in the right places. One thing I do is haggle for the prices as they are not set in stone, and you can get some incredible discounts when you buy in bulk. As I have mentioned, other payments are made for various options, such as jumping the queue for a press release, the ability to edit an article once it has been published or by Domain Authority (DA), which is the website's ranking.

Don't take a rejected pitch to a journalist personally

It's hard to know when you'll be featured in the media, even though you might feel like your story is a priority. There are so many changes taking place in newsrooms as stories get positioned up and down the priority list, and it can feel like rejection. One of my clients got featured through my contribution months after I worked with them. It is important to remember that there are many factors affecting when a story will make airtime, whether it's simply bad timing or due to new developments in a story. Yes, my client was on television weeks after our project was completed; however, I could see the reasoning behind this decision. When I first contacted the television news channel, they were extremely interested in telling my client's story, as evidenced by their Freedom of Information (FOI) request. It was months later that I saw a half-hour special on the television, and there was my client.

Another reason pitches and press releases may be rejected is the type of business or marketing content that is included. I have had clients featured in trade magazines with news items more focused on products and services. When it comes to the media, think about what attracts audiences. As a start-up, it's important to create content that matches the media outlet. There are two key factors this makes me think of; the first is 'clickbait'. This is an intriguing story headline that entices readers to click on a link to a particular web page. However, if your story needs to be stronger, it won't be featured. The second is related to your newsworthiness. If you want to share a story with the press, make sure you haven't shared it on social media before they get their hands on it. There is a detailed list of newsworthy topics in Chapter 4.

Reboot your pitch to get a YES from the journalist

Not every journalist will reject a pitch if you revise it. Sometimes, it is possible to rework a rejected pitch into a successful one by repurposing it. I've sent the same pitch with a personalised message to several contacts, and their reactions have varied. One thing I've learned is that artificial intelligence (AI) can help me with generating ideas for content. I use a platform that can rewrite my text and find email subject lines or create paragraphs from bullet points or titles at the touch of a button. Obviously, I create original content and then use AI to repurpose it again on my website, emails, or social media.

Speed is important in PR and the media. As you know, I am a member of the Chartered Institute of Public Relations (PR). When studying for my CIPR Professional PR Diploma, I followed the breaking news of Prince Harry and Meghan Markle during HRH Queen Elizabeth II's passing. It was almost impossible to keep up with or fact-check the constant updates.

My experience working in PR has strengthened my resolve as a business owner and as a professional. Having a solution is essential to success, and pitching your expertise to people who can spot potential in you is a valuable experience. For example, when I was accepted into the NatWest Entrepreneur Accelerator program at the University of Warwick, I knew I must have something of value to offer and scale up in my business. The PR side of this meant that I could associate myself with their decision. The media affects me in a similar way by holding up a mirror to what I am doing, which gives me valuable reflection time. As a start-up, you may have many ideas that could be better once they are in the public eye. As you have seen, I had to change my business name at short notice, only days before my new website was built, and the domain name needed to be decided.

5 tips for mastering rejection and overcoming it with resilience

In the early months of developing my business, I revisited my business plan. I'm not going to lie; I had completely forgotten what it contained. The forms, documents, business model canvas and headache of prospective cash flow made me wince. I started my self-employment journey in 2018 with a scattergun approach, and I was determined not to rinse and repeat this process when I started Little PR Rock Marketing in 2020. This meant devising a new business plan.

I tried several value propositions for this idea. As I spoke about my ideas on a live streamlined TV channel and watched the interviewers' surprise and delight, I knew I had something unique to offer. I tell you this because rejection can come in many different forms. It may be a side glance from someone face to face, outright derision about your ideas, or a flat "No" or a "Not yet." Others may beat you to the media, and you become old news, but the one thing you have is the resilience to bounce back. None of the above rejections feels quite so bad to me as I write this, as I have learned from every one of them. I once owned a book called 'SAS. Are You Tough Enough?' Latterly there have been times I think I am. I now look for those side glances or the rise of an eyebrow when someone is impressed. That helps me to decide what works and what I need to improve.

Resilience is like a muscle we exercise by putting ourselves in challenging situations in order to spring back our emotional and physical elasticity, making us stronger. We become more elastic when we learn how to bounce back from setbacks so we can move forward with confidence and purpose. Resilience is an ability comic-book characters often acquire in order to become more malleable when dealing with their lives both in and out of their costumes. As business owners, we may not wear a comic disguise, but we do understand how that must feel. We are often both public and private personas. The show always goes on!

I have identified the five important conditions of my life that demonstrate to me the overall status of my ability to bounce back. This breakdown provides a birds-eye view, puts me in control of my life and can create a sense of my future-paced self.

- Emotional well-being: Trust your past experiences to help you cope with another upheaval
- Inner drive: Rely on your ability to stay positive and find alternative solutions

- Positive relationships: Make those who lift you up the focus of your world and reciprocate.
- Purpose: Remember, at your core, is the beginning of a new chapter in your life.
- Physical health: Nourish your mind from the inside out with food that calms the soul.

While many people may consider the idea of starting a business during a COVID-19 pandemic to be crazy, I knew that once I had come to terms with losing my liberty and adapted to my concerns about my emotional health, creativity would surely follow. Now with this book, I can help you to get media exposure, to stack that coverage and repurpose that content to impress and convert potential clients. I am developing a PR agency with a freelance team offering support to do your own PR or we can provide done-for-you assets, including pitching to the media, press releases, ghostwriting and media kits. I have achieved this as the same person who was rejected outside that nightclub. PR, to me, also stands for perseverance and resilience. That is now my superpower!

So, what did the IPO Trade Mark office say about my business name?

Examination of Trade Mark Application

Your application does not appear to meet the requirements for registration for the following reason.

The summary of the assessor's 'Absolute grounds for refusal'.

The term "The Visuals Adviser" is not registrable as a Trade Mark. Such a mark is likely to be required by other undertakings in the ordinary course of their trade, thus inconveniencing them. The addition of "the" would indicate that this company is the only or best one providing such services within the United Kingdom.

The proposed trademark, "The Visuals Adviser", does not suggest any unique qualities of your services. To be considered distinctive and capable of distinguishing your goods from those of another undertaking, a mark should have an element that is unique to you and sets you apart from others in the marketplace.

Fair points and a valuable lesson in IP and rejection.

CHAPTER 7

Unlocking the Power of PR

PR Is the Perfect Marketing Fit for Your Start-up: Here's Why

Public relations and publicity - what is the difference?

Public relations and publicity are not the same, but the two often overlap. Publicity does not attempt to sway public opinion in any specific direction. It simply draws the attention of the public towards something. As we have established, PR encompasses all activities that might influence the opinion that others have of your business. Added to this, advertisements can be ignored by consumers who feel bombarded by marketing messages every day, which means that managed wisely, PR can be more cost-effective than advertising.

In this chapter, I will share my biggest takeaways after nearly 25 years of working in the communications field and as a developing business owner. Over the years, I found that PR carries a level of authority and trust that traditional marketing cannot provide.

1. **Note the difference between your marketing and PR messages.**

    Marketing message: "I am a PR & Communications Strategist thought leader in the Midlands."

    That is a marketing message, and it is very effective in its impact. After telling you this, the copy I write afterwards might continue with memorable and catchy phrases to describe what I do. There may be a paragraph on why I do what I do, a bombardment of my expertise and a passage which is authentic in its vulnerability and my need to connect with you.

PR message: "PR Start-up Celebrates Winning Second Place in Global PR Industry Awards"

If you saw this headline, what would you think? The article would explain that these Public Relations Today MVP Awards 2022 are "designed to recognise the most useful, actionable, and well-written thought leadership in our content community, as determined by their judges and readers."

That credible news story may be the decision-maker that gains your trust. It is that simple.

2. Invest in PR early - to get the best results!

When I set out in my PR business, I began to lay foundations which started to take effect in the following months and then years. The article I won second place with was published in *Prowly*, a PR industry blog, in January 2022. It was only at the end of the year, in November 2022, I discovered I had the chance to win an award for it. Now I get to tell you about it too. Writing a thought leadership article is demanding, especially when I lacked confidence then. This article may not have happened if I had given into doubt. Here is the backstory.

I had met with a potential client who had been referred to me. They had gained much media attention after an event that had gone viral online. I was keen to learn more, and during a Zoom meeting, we established they were managing their PR affairs themselves, and it had been exciting yet time-consuming. As part of my due diligence, I researched their media exposure, and it was escalating. However, for me, the message they wanted to convey was being diluted through appearances and articles purely for entertainment purposes. I was early in my business and naïve enough to write a very thorough proposal that I thought would help this potential client regain control of their media exposure. I was unsuccessful in landing that client, but the article this experience inspired became a finalist in those PR awards. It was called, 'Media Overexposure: How to Take Back Control of Your Media Presence'. I can proudly announce "I am a PR & Communications Strategist thought leader in the Midlands" in the media. That is the power of thought leadership and PR together.

3. A rise of integrity in the PR industry?

The public's perception of PR is on the upswing, but it hasn't always been that way. Back in the day, it wasn't uncommon for PR professionals to get ahead of bad press and spin the story in such a way that absolved their client of any guilt. PR has recovered from its tarnished reputation, but only after going through a lot. It took time, but the industry has learned that it can rise above this by staying true to its integrity. To do so, they have had to get rid of some of the old ways of doing things, such as exaggerating stories.

Many PR professionals aren't willing to sacrifice their integrity for their clients anymore and are using new practices that keep them honest. As a result, the public's perception of PR has turned around and become much more positive than it once was. The rise of social media has had a huge impact on the public relations industry. The negative attention the PR industry received due to spinning is what forced these tactics out, replacing them with more promising (and ethical) methods like reputation and crisis management. Once again, this proves the media's power in moulding our industries and giving audiences a say in how they want brands to communicate.

There are many types of PR communications, including media relations, strategic communications, community relations, crisis communications, internal employee communications, public affairs, and online and social media. Every one of these will find its place as you develop your business, but when we start out, there are elements we can begin to master from the outset that is 'lower hanging fruit.' I focus on guest posting, radio and speaking engagements, networking, LinkedIn, and national or sometimes global media pitching. Your route will depend on where you need to be visible to your audience and where you feel confident. Here is a non-exhaustive list of possibilities for you to be heard.

16 ways to make the most of your PR activities

- Press releases
- Speaking engagements
- Social media engagement
- Community events
- Partnering with influencers
- Leverage testimonials
- Feature in editorials
- Backlinks
- Market research
- Becoming an author
- Guest posting

- Memberships
- Awards
- Pitching to journalists
- Networking
- Event management

4. The fuss about guest posting and Digital PR?

As PR adapts to the new online media, its role includes plenty of copywriting and relationship building. Marketing strategies focus on customers and generating leads to make sales. PR, as I explained, is concerned with all stakeholders, media, and the public at large. "Digital PR" has become a norm and embraces online media, including websites, social media, search engine optimisation (SEO), Google guidelines and content creation. When combined with offline marketing strategies, digital PR and marketing can be effective ways to improve online presence and visibility by connecting with a qualified audience to spread news and information much more rapidly than would otherwise be possible.

As mentioned, online PR campaigns are easier to measure than traditional PR campaigns. Indeed, digital campaigns can be tracked and monitored, allowing for clear reporting that demonstrates the return on investment (ROI). Little PR Rock Marketing focuses on improving our clients' digital footprint to create a legacy of media coverage that will last a lifetime, if not longer. After many years of experience supporting charities and galleries, I now embrace digital PR.

Traditionally a strong digital PR strategy includes writing and publishing high-quality articles on websites with a high Domain Authority (DA) that have backlinks to a brand's website. National press and magazines, local newspapers, and business and industry-related media still have high-ranking websites. You may not get paid for your contributions to these media, so there is nothing to lose in asking for a backlink. Keep in mind that the nature of backlinks is now changing. Creating high-quality content is important to any successful business today. As business owners, we are constantly working to improve our content offerings, and we want our clients to feel confident that the content they receive from us is the very best it can be. These valuable messages are shared in all our marketing, including PR. In the digital world, where brands are more transparent than ever and reputations can be damaged by a single social media post, digital PR can be hugely beneficial to a brand.

5 Reasons Your Business Needs Digital PR

- PR helps to grow website traffic by getting the company in front of potential customers, or it may attract investors through editorial coverage
- A third-party platform can introduce your company to new audiences. A digital public relations strategy builds your brand by increasing the online mentions of your organisation
- Digital PR is often free, creating an online footprint that can be seen globally so that your content is appreciated in different ways, with long-lasting coverage and ROI.
- Think of digital PR as improving your website's SEO - search engine optimisation. Google was founded as a hypertextual search engine. Backlinks are a key component to how websites appear in search engine results pages
- Using digital PR is a way to build trust with consumers. The more they trust your brand, the more likely they are to buy what you're selling

5. Talk about what makes you feel passionate

After 30 years of experience in mental health services from the inside and the outside as a Community Mental Health Worker for several years, it may not surprise you that I decided to become a Rethink Media Volunteer. Rethink aims to improve the lives of people affected by mental illness and ensure they have a good quality of life. I feel passionate about their charity cause. I attended several local PR events and contributed to their national magazine once or twice during my time as a graphic designer and at the recovery house.

This experience made me realise I could make a difference that went beyond a financial gain and is why I have worked so hard for several charities, businesses and galleries. It also made me happy to hear from a recruitment consultant that she would have loved my Curriculum Vitae (CV) or resume when I was out of work.

I try not to say "No" to opportunities when they arise. It is important to know your limitations and mentally trial how you will cope with an event. Now when people ask to quote me in articles and press releases, I am keen to help. That ability to add value is my motivation rather than a personal appraisal. It is only after 30 years that the time is right for me to speak to the media on this subject of mental health. PR is about being both passionate and ready to get involved. Ten years as a Media Officer enabled me to leverage PR for my business; now, I can help others too.

6. It's time to consider PR events

PR can be a very high-profile activity, so being confident to respond as an expert in your industry and staying on topic will be beneficial for you at the time and when sharing your experiences later in the media. When star-studded events are included in your marketing strategy, PR enables you to elevate your business through association with VIP attendees and exclusive hospitality (or prominence).

Planning events can be difficult. I've seen invitations go astray; my personal favourite was the cupboard of branded t-shirts that were stored with all the small t-shirts at the back and the large at the front. If they had been stored randomly, everyone would have received a shirt that fit. Instead, those at the back of the line got small shirts regardless of their size because all the large shirts had been given out. I can smile now in hindsight, but I have learned a valuable lesson.

Here are some more tips I have learned over the years working during PR events with several charities, art galleries and businesses that you may find to help you on your thought leadership path in raising your profile at PR events.

- **Be mindful of the media attending your PR event**

I remember having the role of taking care of the performance artists at one event as they entertained the people in the town with their quirky antics. I had several to monitor, and it was fun to see the children interacting. Then for a moment, I got distracted, and one of the troupe disappeared from my view. I panicked a little inside, wondering what I was going to do. "They can't be hard to find?" I thought. Suddenly I was in company. The man next to me came closer. I turned and remarked, "I have lost my Strangeling", which was the performers' name. "Oh dear", said the man. "I am [name] from The Times." "Oh, you don't say?" I stuttered and then crumpled and sped off, feeling caught out.

The next time I was cautious was when the television news crews arrived. I was a smoker then and left the building in a hurry in need of a cigarette. Cameras were waiting outside for me, and all I could think was that my mother would be horrified to see me smoking on the news! I took a detour and found a hiding place. I am glad I do not smoke now because of examples like this.

- **Anticipate the questions the media may ask**

One of the reasons I provide my clients with ten questions and answers the media may ask is so they are more prepared in an emergency. The media do like to probe with newsworthy angles. Many years ago, I was interviewed by BBC radio, and I was coping rather well, I thought. I was in a false sense of security when the interviewer asked for details that were beyond me. Rather flustered, I waved my hands frantically in front of me to stop the conversation. Highly unprepared and unprofessional. Sometimes you may have an idea of the questions you will be asked, and the interview is fluid and more relaxing. After one news interview on a live-streaming TV channel, I remember it going well, and at the end, when I should have already left, he said, "Well, that was nice." I took that as a compliment. I'm "nice".

- **Be flexible with your event timings**

If you are reaching out to a celebrity, royalty, or the media, you need to understand that they have busy diaries and are visiting your organisation at their convenience. Having a set date for your event may need to have wiggle room for their benefit. When you speak or write to their representatives, it is important to be specific and show a genuine interest in their work. You may wait some time for a response. You could have a missed call on your answerphone (it does happen), so make sure that you are enthusiastic about their attendance and can offer an incentive rather than the cost per mile for their petrol to get to your event. Remember that everyone is equal, and that VIPs respond to authenticity when they are included as such. HRH King Charles III is a great example of a monarch with a sense of humour.

- **Research who you are working with**

There is nothing worse than being unprepared at PR events. Not knowing who you are talking to is a recipe for disaster. Many years ago, I received a phone call inviting me to take part in a magazine photoshoot and confused the hairdresser's name with a radio presenter. Despite doing my homework, I was still concerned about making the same mistake in person. Knowing the importance of the photographer made me respectful, even as the propeller fans blew at me, and I moved awkwardly from shot to shot.

On another occasion, I was in a refreshment queue with a gallery owner who I spoke to rather candidly until I realised who he was. I knew that my being outspoken needed to be addressed, so now I practise public speaking. I record myself online so that I can spot the tangents where I wander off and rein them back on stage and during interviews. I cannot underestimate the benefits of public speaking for confidence in all forms of communication.

One time I attended an event without research and felt rather foolish. During the meet and greet with one celebrity, I said, "How great to meet you. You are an inspiration." We then posed for the obligatory selfie photograph. Only moments later, the same celebrity took to the stage and began her speech. Within minutes she tackled the subject of her challenges, saying, "I don't like to be called inspirational much." I wanted to find the nearest exit.

- **It's not all about high-tech equipment**

When interviewed by the local radio once, I was so concerned about saying "the right thing" that I had a script, despite only speaking for minutes. When the piece was recorded, it was shot on a mobile phone outdoors for ease, but the result was upside down for some unknown reason. I laughed off the many attempts I took to answer the simplest questions, so now I know what I can and cannot say. That means during the interview and 'off the record', as I don't think there really is an 'off the record' conversation these days. I always say that if I am not prepared to tell the nation on a celebrity chat show, then I do not say it publicly on air or online.

The second time I was surprised was a radio recording on an iPad. I had always imagined cameras and crew for every occasion, but this relaxed approach seems to be a norm now as we are all familiar with the technology. I have recorded interviews this way myself, and the only snag can sometimes be the sound quality which can be resolved with an external directional microphone.

It is also not uncommon to receive a phone interview with a journalist from a national newspaper, so you need to be ready. There may also be unexpected glitches in tech that you have not accounted for but need to master live on air. During one live news interview, my computer camera failed to connect. I was talking about creativity, so an image of someone making a ceramic pot appeared on the screen as I stumbled over the words, "Can you hear me?" The rest of the interview took place with that image in place. I have never successfully thrown a ceramic pot as an artist, so it did make me smile.

- **Learn how to hold your nerve**

When you attend PR events or address the media, it can be nerve-wracking. I remember serving coffee to the press. There were so many of them filtering in, and as I pushed down the plunger of the cafeteria, I shook, and it twisted, leaking coffee grinds into the hot water. There have been many occasions when I stuttered and stammered internally, but it did not show to others.

The media can often throw you a curveball, so when you think you are being interviewed to speak about a particular topic, they ask you something completely unrelated. This has happened to me several times. Whilst on the radio, I talked about my business planning course rather than the book I was promoting and struggled to get back on track. It is wise not to be too obvious about having an agenda with a presenter. Going live is the most pressurised situation; however, with practice, you can master the process, building up your confidence from local to national and global media.

CHAPTER 8

Become A Chief Reputation Officer

PR Tips That Could Make or Break Your Start-up Growth

What happens when you are in too many places at once?

As I have said, the key to PR is getting yourself the most beneficial media exposure possible. You must find ways to know where your name needs to be for public consumption and at what times, places, and forums. These days getting featured can create a ripple effect where your comments can go viral. Therefore, what about the effects of your frequency of publicity? Can overexposure have a detrimental effect?

For me, the answer is yes. Overexposure is when a message or product receives too much media coverage, resulting in the audience losing interest in the message. It is considered an exception rather than a rule but may result from the excessive interaction of all media messages. Thankfully, it may not be as damaging as you think. Having a strategy is essential when overexposure begins to occur and can help you maintain control over your media coverage and prevent audience burnout.

Steps to avoid over-exposure in the media

There are several ways to avoid overexposure in the media. For example, before you even think about riding the next wave of press, it's important to examine your current level of exposure and measure its impact on your publicity. List the steps involved in your publicity campaigns. Assess and analyse your media coverage to produce results you can measure. Identify the best opportunities to engage with the media in the future using various techniques. You may need to consider and record any hype around your name, benchmark the results of campaigns, get ownership of assets where possible, and find mentions of your name so that you can protect it as exposure begins to escalate.

Media outlets know that their audiences like to see people they recognise, so they strive to provide a proportion of familiarity in their publicity. While there is nothing wrong with seeing familiar faces once in a while, too much exposure can lead to audience boredom and decreased interest in what they have to say. When you get a peak in publicity, don't be afraid to actively seek opportunities based on the connections you will have already made. You may manage a peak in publicity more naturally when you have loyal relationships with the media and your audience.

To avoid overwhelm, choose appearances and interviews to help you increase your know, like, and trust factor. Maximise your impact by limiting your availability. This approach requires cherry-picking interviews and appearance requests for maximum value. The decision of what offers to accept, or decline is up to you. You will be more likely to be asked for your opinion if you add value and stay on topic without obvious repetition. If you want to remain credible, avoid giving the impression that you are concerned about overexposure.

Mastering the PR cycle of staying on topic

To create a sustainable reputation, you need to understand your target audience. Audiences today receive information in different ways and react to it differently than audience members in the past. If you want to create maximum impact, save yourself from exhaustion, and get the best return on your investment, focus on media outlets that specialise in your topic if you feel that you are becoming overexposed by mainstream media outlets.

Negative publicity can be avoided by allowing your message to reach a positive peak before returning for another cycle. The trick is to know when to stay in the background as part of a structured effort. Laying low maintains the clarity of your message and coordinated consistency across all channels, including local press and all forms of online media.

Good PR is about saying the same thing with fresh new perspectives that engage with your stakeholders. Successful public figures focus on their areas of expertise and create powerful messages that stick in people's minds. The best message statements are fact-based, appealing, understandable to your audience and memorable. This can boost your reputation as an expert in your field. Experts can influence the entire industry's direction, inspire others to innovate and become role models for the people around them.

Once you have gained a large amount of media exposure, decide what goals you aim to achieve by pursuing further PR and what happens next. Consider every aspect of communicating a message; for example, in addition to deciding how you want your message to be framed, you must also determine who will be communicating it, especially in a crisis situation.

CEOs are not spectators in a PR crisis

A PR crisis can make or break any business. If you experience an unexpected crisis, your next PR campaign will become a virtual blueprint for any future communications and media coverage. Media exposure is a complex, delicate process. When a crisis strikes, it's an all-hands-on-deck moment to prevent the situation from spiralling out of control. I am not a crisis communications expert yet, but I do understand that your CEO brand could be the saviour of your business in times of crisis.

As CEO, you are the voice of your business, both internally and externally.

As the world becomes increasingly connected and transparent, CEOs have more opportunities to take a stand on issues that matter to them, their employees, and their customers. This highlights the need for your 'Internal Reputation Compass', which affects your behaviour as a CEO. As I've said, customers don't just buy based on a product or service; they buy into the company itself.

As a start-up, your personal brand is a work in progress. As CEOs become more accessible through social media accounts, they have more opportunities to build their profiles and connect with their audience on a more personal level. As a result, CEOs need to invest serious time into their personal branding, which is crucial during crises.

Becoming a crisis spokesperson is no easy task

You can manage a crisis by not overcompensating and making too many public statements. Often, well-crafted information given by a company spokesperson will be enough. As a start-up, that spokesperson may well be you as the business founder and upcoming CEO. Having prepared quotes available to the media, as well as professional commentary, helps to offset negative comments made by others. However, when you over-communicate, you ask for targeted criticism from your audience because they will dig even deeper into your work, looking for mistakes.

If you do have spokespeople, they need to be resourceful under pressure. They need to be quick on their feet, and they need to know how to communicate effectively. They should be empathetic and genuine when dealing with people with questions or concerns about a crisis. They need in-depth knowledge of the situation and to present a unified front for your company.

A crisis management team can help put these pieces into place for you. This group of people selected due to their expertise and speciality in different aspects of the business stand behind the spokesperson. They need to be available 24/7 in times of crisis. Should a spokesperson need advice and information that needs to be relayed to the stakeholders, it can be done by this team rather than having the CEO try to do it alone. Having this support system in place will help you avoid missteps so you can deal confidently with any unexpected problems that come up.

You cannot control the media, but you can influence them

The ability to control the news cycle is best exemplified by staying on message, sticking to a positive and controlled tone, and working to cultivate relationships with journalists. As I said, many people believe they can control the media by controlling what they say to journalists. In the end, journalists need to do whatever makes them money.

If you're the first to set the tone of new stories, you'll be able to understand the news and industry dialogue better than anyone else. With a first-hand understanding of a situation, you should be able to update your media distribution plan accordingly. Media exposure is a delicate matter that requires thoughtful consideration. It is important to show your message repeatedly in the marketplace, but not so often that consumers become bored with it.

Personal branding is the mind that drives your company brand

My personal brand is paramount. I am always aware of it and aspire to build a strong one. I had a ten-year career as a Media Officer at a charity, including managing their external crisis media communications during the lockdown caused by the COVID-19 pandemic. I am now self-employed and have been helping clients think about how they can brand themselves as authorities, thought leaders and go-to experts and improve their personal and business brands through PR. As experts and thought leaders, we must see what's coming in the business world and demonstrate we have access to data that allows them to make informed decisions. Such a reputation will enhance our personal brands when disaster strikes. I suggest that an ability to delegate, make recommendations and demonstrate that you are familiar with data enhances your Credibility Confidence.

Business experts need a reputation for listening to the best advice and doing the right thing. The CEO needs to develop a business's thought leadership strategy. The CEO becomes the 'mind' of the company. The 'mind' creates a vision statement that drives the company. Vision is, by its very nature, a human quality. Personal branding requires a vision, just like the company brand. Our ability to see into the future and take a long-term view sets us apart from other creatures. We may not get everything right, but as people, our ability to plan and make choices about what matters most to us is a defining feature. Personal branding provides reassurance in a crisis because it provides an essential human element.

A CEO connects to social purpose on a deeper human level than a business. As I said, Millennials, in particular, are increasingly interested in buying from businesses with a clear social purpose. However, what if it is not just Millennials? What if we are all increasingly interested in buying from businesses with a clear social purpose? In times of crisis, opinions can be polarising. Your personal brand needs to have the reputation of someone who keeps providing as much useful information as possible to add to the conversation.

It's important to understand what attracts and repels people in order to create your personal brand. You need to take steps as your CEO to equip yourself for crises. Having an opinion that attracts and repels is the basis of all relationships, and business relationships are no exception. There's no better way to set the tone for your company than by doing it yourself. It's crucial that your actions support your message and drive goodwill between people, but it's also vital that your voice be consistent with your 'message' and your actions. When a crisis strikes, you will be leading from the front, so it's essential that you are presentable both physically and emotionally.

Build trust in your brand: By telling it like it is and being accountable

Trust is a human condition, and as you can see, your personal brand speaks volumes. Your message must reflect your core mission and value statement in every action and reaction during a crisis. It makes no difference if you are a start-up, a small business owner, or a CEO of a large corporation – your ability to resonate with your stakeholders will be a marker to judge your actions. In a crisis, your stakeholders need to hear from you. Your ability to communicate with your stakeholders will determine how well you handle crises. They need to know the truth about what has happened and what will happen going forward.

They also need to know that you take full responsibility for the problem and have an action plan to fix it. You will need to take ownership of the problem or situation, show that you understand what happened and why you commit to a solution and timeline for resolution, and ensure that everyone knows the person accountable for the fix and how it will get done. Goodwill is the foundation of relationships, and it drives actions and reactions. If you have goodwill with your customers, they will react positively to you when you make mistakes. They will be more forgiving, but first, you need to earn their trust.

Personal branding has become a fact of life. CEOs are now constantly managing the impressions others have about them, sometimes consciously and sometimes unconsciously. Just to recap, when you become a CEO, it's no longer just about you. Your words and actions reflect on you and your company, your investors, and your employees. You must be conscious of how others will perceive everything you do. Anyone can share every message, tweet, or email with millions of people worldwide before you know what has happened.

Some best practices for communicating in a crisis

- **What's the best way to create a positive presence?**

  For every business, effective communication is critical, but it is especially important for CEOs and other high-profile executives. Your employees, business partners, and customers look to you for guidance.

- **What content will you use to populate channels?**

  You need to be proactive and take the lead to ensure that your communications reflect your company's values and show empathy towards those affected by the crisis.

- **What is the best way to tell your story?**

  When posting on your company's behalf, ensure you're sharing information with care. Don't assume that people are familiar with your company's position on the issue. Keep focusing on helping others through your message rather than promoting your brand.

There will always be plenty of criticism, but criticism is just an opinion. A CEO who can deal with criticism has a strong understanding of his or her core values and can demonstrate this through consistent daily actions. Leading during a crisis requires focusing on your fundamental mission and delivering confidence in your value statement; this will differentiate you from everyone else, who may criticise but never provide solutions when needed most. You will be the guide for your employees. My own personal brand as an entrepreneur includes a clear vision, shared beliefs, and a spirit of adventure; these elements will help you lead your employees to great things.

Be a 'Brand for Good' by combining your business with social impact

Humanity had not seen anything like the COVID-19 pandemic before. While our lives were disrupted beyond measure by this virus, it also created opportunities for us to use our creativity, resourcefulness, and resilience to come up with ways to help people navigate this crisis.

Businesses are increasingly integrating their brands with social impact. Social impact is any positive change in society that solves or addresses social injustices and challenges. Currently, purpose rather than profit is becoming the business rationale. This way of thinking is essential to your personal brand. You need to articulate what your business stands for and how it contributes to the world to attract exceptional talent, build lasting customer relationships, and make an enduring contribution to society. By acknowledging social impact and committing to creating a fairer, sustainable future, your company fosters a brand and culture that rewards innovation and incentivises positive behaviours. Our stakeholders will scrutinise our values and purpose in a crisis.

To successfully implement social impact initiatives, you need to understand how you and your business contribute to society or whatever cause you choose to support. You must also create a clear vision of how you want your company's culture to look for social impact, considering all stakeholders' interests (e.g., your employees, customers, investors etc.). Your business brand should show that you align with the social issues you want to address through the business model; this is also known as your "Why". It needs to be grounded within the industry in which your company operates.

Remember, audiences respect brands with a social purpose, that are ethically minded, or donate to charitable causes and sponsor initiatives that improve human lives or help those less fortunate. A responsibility to the environment, ethical and human rights issues, philanthropy, and economic matters demonstrates that you have strong values. Today words like 100% Natural Origin, Organic, Vegan, Cruelty-Free, Handmade, Halal, No Palm Oil, No Parabens, No Toxins, No Fragrance and No GM Ingredients have profound significance. Remember: In PR, altruism and a humanistic attitude pay back, not just because it's the right thing to do, but because it makes you feel good too. Base your news story to ethically boost your reputation rather than to make headlines for maximum impact for your business. I must stress here that social purpose must come from a place of genuine altruism; no one wants to be deceived by PR spin.

Reputation management is a critical aspect of any brand

The power dynamics have shifted in favour of the consumer as they choose to do business with a company or not based on how they feel about its brand reputation. 'Reputation management' is more important than ever. We live in a 'cancel culture' where our customers can block us out and 'cancel' us instantly at any given time. The world has evolved, and therefore PR must develop. PR needs to be about creating disruptive content for your business that will cut through all the noise and keenly understand how its customers and stakeholders perceive it.

Here are your three relevant reputations below. All these types of reputation are very important for success as a start-up because you are creating the foundations for your business with each carefully considered step:

Character reputation is how you behave towards customers. It makes up an important part of your business's overall personality, too (including its values and culture, for example) and is an important aspect for potential customers to consider.

Capability reputation is based on the knowledge and judgments of others regarding an individual's abilities in a given area. These include personal characteristics, education, training, experience, and skills. While individuals may feel they know what kind of person they are, the truth is that most people don't really know them well enough to form a solid opinion about their capabilities. The only way to get a firm grasp on what a person can do (or not) is through interactions with that person and talking to others who are familiar with them.

Outcome reputation is based on the knowledge and judgments of others regarding how successfully a person has achieved certain goals and objectives in the past. It encompasses all the successes and failures that have occurred throughout an individual's career thus far. Outcome reputation is also based on the outcomes related to any projects or initiatives an individual has overseen or led in the past.

The fact is that PR is crucial for all of us; we all have a reputation, just as I did outside that nightclub. Rejection is inevitable in PR as we all search for the same media coverage at a time when journalists are working harder than ever. Our expertise fuels the media stories of tomorrow, and all we have to do is become that trusted source of information and have the skills to communicate effectively. PR is just part of your marketing strategy these days, but it is one of the most important.

Remember: Don't let your mistakes spiral into a PR nightmare

As a start-up, you must prepare in advance for various potential crises, including extreme weather, crime, cyber-attacks, product recalls, corporate wrongdoing, reputation crises and PR incidents. Your business will be better able to respond swiftly and effectively to each crisis if you have laid out a plan beforehand. Here are some points to consider:

Employees are your most valuable asset in a crisis

In times of crisis, people are more important than profits. If a crisis strikes your business, you should be honest with your employees and keep them fully informed. When things get tough, leaders must lead by example. They should stay calm, communicate clearly, and show compassion to their staff members.

As Vineet Nayar writes in his book "Employees First, Customers Second: Turning conventional management upside down" (2010), employees are valuable stakeholders because they are financially dependent on their employers. Employees have a more substantial emotional commitment and often stay longer than customers. Understanding staff also helps bring authenticity; communicating honestly with your workforce is critical for employee well-being during periods of crisis when uncertainty can lead to anxiety.

It is crucial to reassure employees that they will get through this together while remaining authentic and genuine. Your reputation as CEO with your employees is built or broken in a crisis, so an established firm footing before the crisis will help. Employees want to feel secure, so the more confident you appear, the better your chance of winning their trust. When you don't focus on your PR and reputation management, you can be seen as shallow and only interested in sales.

Crisis does not need to be negative.

The COVID-19 pandemic was a painful time for many of us, including me. Working from home for the charity meant I made decisions about what to include in media relations more autonomously because I could not pop into a colleague's office to double-check my competency. We weathered the storm together. However, I also realised, "I can do this more independently than I have done in the past," and my opinion was not unfounded. That is how Little PR Rock Marketing was born in the middle of the UK lockdown crisis in 2020. I had no idea what I was capable of, my perception of myself was skewed, and I would never have found out if the crisis had not happened. Everyone I knew had faith in me.

Consider hiring a PR firm and making an investment in your brand

You must test and quickly learn how to create your PR habits when you start up. You need to be ready to roll with the punches of an emergency situation and keep your head up while the media asks tough questions. However, when you can commit to the costs, learn to delegate, and outsource parts of the business, including the ones you are not an expert at or that someone else can do more quickly than you.

You'll need to do PR for some time to know what your employees and freelancers will do. It may not seem like it now, but scaling your business requires you to hire the best people you can for each role. Some people might baulk at the idea of spending the money on an outside PR firm. Still, in the long run, if you really want to make a good impression on everyone, your employees, and your customers who talk about you, you're going to have to take every step necessary to make sure that things go as smoothly as possible.

HOW TO BUY
MULTIPLE COPIES OF THIS BOOK

You can bulk-order this book for training purposes.

Please get in touch with Abbi directly at Little PR Rock Marketing with your details and shipping address to let us know where to mail multiple copies. Buying several copies will create a discount on the price of each book. All you need to do is pay for the shipping and the new cost of the books, and they will soon be on their way to you.

Please order in quantities:

10 copies
20 copies
30 copies

For large quantities
further arrangements
can be made.

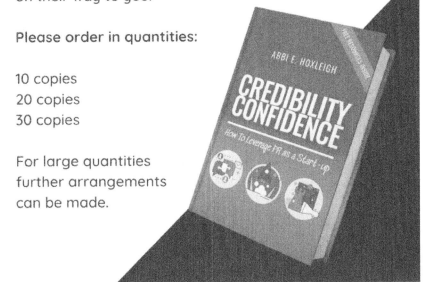

CHAPTER 9

Discover Your Inner Expert

The Secret to Building Credibility Confidence as an Expert

There are times in our lives when we wonder who we are and what is the point of our existence. When I started, my business pivoted, and I developed Little PR Rock Marketing. That gives me purpose. It also gives me an identity. When I look back to my teens, I remember the person I was then and how confusing the world around me was at that time. There always seemed to be something in someone else's life that was greener than in mine. However, by focusing on building my Credibility Confidence, I can communicate better and find opportunities that I would never have dreamed of coming my way. For example, going from writing to public speaking has enabled me to provide training in PR and Credibility Confidence. I use the same principles as the workshops, boot camps and training I enjoyed, including small groups of no more than ten people, a series of exercises and conversations and listening to others' experiences.

I remember standing on the stage at Coombe Abbey at the Woman Who Achieves Awards on 1st October 2021 was the most exhilarating and terrifying experience. After months of lockdowns, it was incredible to be around so many people networking again. My excitement meant that when I took my place to speak, I delivered with great confidence. That was a moment I will never forget and an opportunity for which I am very grateful. I did not realise that there were 160 people in the room and even more simultaneously online.

This was the keynote that I needed to tell. My own personal journey of struggling with my identity until I found my confidence and purpose. This was the personal story within me that I needed to expel to continue public speaking.

I was then prepared for my educational keynotes in 2022. The first was for the Federation of Small Businesses (FSB) at their Business Bootcamp and Networking event. I never intended to become a public speaker. Still, after 18 months of online speaking at networking events during the COVID-19 lockdown as well as this accomplishment in October, there is no going back. This was when I realised my own Credibility Confidence and knew I had shifted my identity for a growth mindset.

6 ways to get personal development right as an entrepreneur

As an entrepreneur, you must continually develop your mindset to get a competitive edge. This can be done by creating a culture of personal and professional development. My learning is more personally meaningful when it is driven by self-direction and motivation. Professional development enables me to gain skills and knowledge through information, reflection, evaluation, application, and analysis to embed its long-term value.

Like detecting the gaps in the market filled by our products and services, we see skills gaps within us that need resolving. As an academic myself, I understand the power of education and personal development as I build my new business in the creative world of PR and marketing. I have discovered six key learning opportunities which impacted me emotionally, upgraded my mindset and changed my behaviour forever. When we gain a combination of sought-after qualifications, relevant experience, and self-education, learning can be fast-tracked and flow more naturally. Here are six cost-effective learning opportunities that could change your life and give you that competitive edge.

Business Coaching

I began my business journey with group coaching online in 2018 and soon discovered that the main barrier to my success was myself. As I reset my money mindset and challenged my past, beliefs, and core values, I became less overwhelmed and maintained my feelings of excitement as I updated my skills and knowledge in all areas of my business.

As my business connections grew, I met more coaches and mentors who showed me how to shift my mindset with a combination of learning styles. My preferred learning style includes a balance of how-to videos, peer-grouping, imitation, reading, audio recordings and taking handwritten notes. A year with a good business coach can keep you accountable and motivated while accelerating your growth rate and directly impacting your sales figures. It can also be cost-effective in the long term because accelerated growth directly impacts sales and productivity.

Webinars

With so many people providing 'how-to' content, free webinars are inevitable. Watching a webinar, I can see if I share the same values as the host and whether I know, like, and trust the information they give me. This learning format can initially feel a little overwhelming because a webinar can be a sales opportunity, with the introduction, some short-win core content, and an offer at the end.

Webinar producers know they can be the bedrock of their multimillion-dollar business, so it is in their interest to give massive value and build lasting relationships with attendees. Free webinars also make great opportunities for 'just-in-time learning' because you will be attracted to a webinar when you need or want more information or to learn something new rather than having a dedicated time and date.

Intuitive Button Pressing

Entrepreneurs need to learn to take risks and 'press buttons' without consciously thinking about how to do it; that's called using your 'intuition'. The skill comes with practice and gaining an understanding of where certain key software elements might be. Technology is often based on utilising the same principles from similar systems well known to the user, making it seem more intuitive.

Using IT software is an important skill for my Continous Professional Development (CPD), as no one wants to be left behind. Technology can help speed up learning and make the process more fun. As entrepreneurs, we learn to take the leap and experiment. Regardless of what technology you are using, knowing that there is a backup enables us to learn by intuitive trial and error.

Immersion

No one can attend a Tony Robbins event such as Unleash the Power Within (UPW) without fully immersing in the process. Since attending UPW, I have memorised and mastered many techniques I learned there. Spending three days with literally thousands of people online in March 2020 changed my life and business beyond recognition.

I created my own self-education course, 'Business Planning for Creative Thinkers: How To Fast Track Your Success As A Creative Entrepreneur', after attending several similar free online events. My course is part of a 'Self-Education Revolution', which entrepreneur

Dean Graziosi coined during Project Next. Many people like myself have joined Mastermind.com to be part of that revolution, a bridge-build between successful and aspiring entrepreneurs.

Other free online courses are available that provide cramming opportunities, such as this UPW, so it is a good idea to subscribe to the email lists of successful entrepreneurs for these events.

Peer Grouping

I surround myself with like-minded people who are as driven as I am, dedicated to making an impact, empowered by the knowledge they have and are ambitious to achieve personal satisfaction as an entrepreneur. This creates a 'mindset collective', which can make learning a shared activity. Pooling our skills and knowledge builds a culture of self-improvement and growth where everyone can improve basic knowledge and turn it into more advanced and complex practices. Learning together also encourages team spirit, where support and nurturing are important to the dynamics of the group.

Reading

Reading can take many forms, from scrolling through Facebook and Instagram to reading a book. Reading is essential to my personal development and helps me grow as a leader. Reading helps me to stay focused and remain intentional about what I learn and how I practise it. Some of the best things to read about include leadership skills and creativity in business, problem-solving techniques, effective communication, conflict resolution, and PR industry knowledge. The internet is a free commodity with many search engines, and social media is a valuable source of information; Kindle books can be relatively inexpensive, and newspapers, magazines and journals give us even more insight into current knowledge.

Education is a continuous process - keep learning!

Personal development is not a one-day course but a process that should be something you engage in daily. Making a habit of professional development and recording achievements can help boost self-esteem, set further goals, and find opportunities to develop in the future by uncovering even more skills gaps. As entrepreneurs, we learn at our own pace and let the seed of curiosity develop. Keeping up with the latest developments in our industry and making sure our qualifications are up to date is crucial. Whether it is traditional or online education programs, educating ourselves is vital to success as entrepreneurs and thought leaders.

As a reminder, thought leaders are those whose ideas and opinions are so respected that people listen to them. They set trends in their industries, inspire others to follow their example, and opportunities fall into their laps. These folks have expertise in their fields and give back to their communities through philanthropy. They constantly seek new ways to improve the world around them. By comparison, leaders focus on improving things in a more tactical sense. They may use a critical or analytical approach to solving problems, but it's all about achieving a certain goal or objective.

Influencers don't necessarily have any expertise of their own; they rely on their ability to persuade others to act or form opinions without needing to go through a rigorous process themselves. Modesty, which is a mindset that focuses on gratitude and self-improvement, will build credibility without self-promotion. The more I learn, the more I realise how little I know.

How to set yourself apart from your peers by gathering insights

To create a distinct and original brand identity, you must first analyse how others have defined their brands, then choose the most effective elements to develop your own. Revolutionary ideas are not always readily accepted, but it is possible to set yourself apart by devising an innovative message that elicits widespread acceptance with the right amount of personalisation.

My clients who don't recognise themselves in their own bios when pitching to the media have just never seen themselves as outsiders would. In my experience, this kind of self-knowledge makes all the difference in the world when it comes to marketing yourself effectively. Remember my client who created her Sofala programme? Using an intellectual framework consistently makes it easier for customers to identify with you and your brand. To establish yourself as a credible source of information and to gain authority, you must create and maintain a robust marketing strategy that reinforces your message.

Given that people have limited time and attention spans online, repurpose your marketing to ensure you're making the most impact in building your brand as an authority in your industry. By staying on top of industry trends, remaining curious about how your industry evolves and approaching your work with a growth mindset, you will ensure that you are always up to date on all things related to your work. A growing understanding of your market niche means you can engage more fluently with people, and their terminology becomes a language for you. However, you may have many areas of expertise as I do because your abilities are transferable.

Here's what happened when I first appeared live on BBC Radio

One of the bravest things I have ever done is appear nationally on BBC Radio. Live on air; you must be ready and forthright and always believe in what you're saying. This is how it happened. When I saw the request on a media request subscription site and Twitter, I knew I could offer some value; I wrote the pitch to the journalist overnight and emailed it eagerly the following day. I followed up by tweeting the journalist to expect a message from me, and within hours as I panicked about finding an email address for my colleague, my inbox became one email fuller. This email was from the BBC journalist; I was so overwhelmed with nervous anxiety as he told me he would call later that day. Undeterred, I gathered myself and messaged back to say I was ready and waiting for his call.

We talked about my experiences, and the journalist said it was similar to others he had spoken to; however, my story had further insight. At the end of the conversation, he said he would like me to be a guest. He explained that I needed to be available between 3 and 3:30 p.m. the following day for a live phone interview and that he would send some questions to me beforehand so I could prepare for being on air during that slot. I was ecstatic, nervous, excited, and thrilled at the same time.

The next day I made notes as I waited for the questions and was patient until they finally arrived just in time. I reworked my answers to fit each question and printed out every line as a bullet point at the journalist's suggestion. Then, I waited for my turn to speak on the radio show. When 3 p.m. arrived, there was no call. I sat with all my notes, began to get slightly tense, and my throat dried up. Suddenly the phone rang from a private number at 3:04 p.m. Asked if I was OK and prepared, I replied that yes, I was ready for anything that came my way. Then, I was told I would join the radio show, where I would hear the guest and host talking before it was my turn to speak.

Another lady was before me, and I wondered if I could distinguish between her name and my own. The journalist on the call spoke to me before I went on air. He made sure he heard my voice clearly before turning on the microphone. He checked that I could hear him and was ready for the interview. The presenter introduced me and began asking me questions about my story and how my experiences had impacted my life. Five minutes felt like seconds. Afterwards, the journalist thanked me for providing my insights on the show and said he would consider me again.

Don't give up on being the best version of yourself

I know how it feels to doubt myself and to feel that I cannot achieve expert status. Many highly successful people have the same sense of 'imposter syndrome'. Being seen and heard by my PR peers was one of the biggest tests. For me, it is an opportunity for personal growth. Why? Because you know that if there are any glitches, they will notice them, and that knowledge gave me the confidence to raise my game and communicate confidently. Times like this are when your passion becomes your focus. There were many other attendees who knew nothing about PR. It can be enough if just one audience member benefits from your words. I can't promise you miracles, but some of the PR I have done in one year has resulted in success for me the following year. I learn, grow, and give back as a rule, and who knows, maybe I'm just one step ahead that will help you too.

The ability to grow and improve as a human being is one of the most important gifts you can give yourself. Personal and professional development can be a tricky subject for some people. On the one hand, it can create a sense of pride and a sense of community with others on the same path as you. On the other hand, you might be used to thinking of yourself in a certain way and changing that self-image can feel unsafe. If you're struggling with something specific, like fear of failure or resistance to change, tackle those issues first. Turning back at any point during your journey towards success can be tempting. Do not give up just because progress is slow or you encounter obstacles along the way; remember, it takes time to build new habits and change old ones.

There are many reasons you should keep pursuing personal development. You cannot expect to be perfect and have everything fall into place after a week or even a month of practice. For example, this book is a great start to learning about PR, but what's next? Some people dive headfirst into guides and videos and go out of their way to buy books on subjects they're interested in, but even with determination, that's not enough for success. You have to put in the effort and discipline yourself to gain experience and stay on track.

Once you feel Credibility Confidence: can you afford yourself?

As start-ups and entrepreneurs, it is important that you develop a human quality to your business through your personal branding, as discussed in Chapter 8. Developing your business brand is essential to your company's PR and marketing strategy. For those just starting their business, it can be tempting to assume you need a specific visual identity before making your first transaction.

As you know, my point of view aligns with Alan Dibb's book 'The One Page Marketing Plan'. Marketing through brand recognition is the realm of major brands as small businesses have limited time or budget to run promotions in sufficient quantities to impact this 'mass marketing' way.

When designing your visual branding, I believe you need to create a starter logo and cost-effective theme for you as a small business owner to grow into. It's like when we tried on shoes when we were children, having our feet measured, walking in the ones we are thinking of buying before purchasing and returning when our feet have grown. Finally, our feet mature, and we walk our path. That insider perspective is how you can analyse your branding and tweak it accordingly. That's how I approach visual branding, mission statements, values and promises to potential customers for start-ups.

Over time, you will grow your business, establish your promise, and gain trust. Your products or services may draw unexpected channels of customers; you may diversify or pivot as you develop your offers and prices. You will build a brand that is a constant loop of information for your niche and subject-matter expertise, and potential thought leadership. Your brand values will align with your potential and existing customers influencing their buying decisions. Find out more about how PR affects your customer journey in Chapter 12.

CHAPTER 10

Getting Into the PR Game

*Build Your Communications Cycle from Marketing and
Sales to Promises*

As you can see, our reputations are not set in stone; we can develop them from Zero to Hero. Not overnight, but step by step from where we are now, no matter where that starting point is. Because the most popular human-interest stories are those of people who achieve despite adversity, we all love rags-to-riches stories because we know they're possible; they inspire us. Your news story is waiting to be told, too; all you need to do is decide what it needs to be.

When my client invested in an 'As Seen in Women's Health' statement, this tells potential clients (and competitors) that her products are allocated in the appropriate place. She essentially piggybacks on the reputation of the magazine. If you have faith that you are the right person, with the right solution, at the right time and at the right price, nothing will stop you! The result of being seen in the media reinforces this statement, just like a referral does to your reputation.

How PR becomes essential in your marketing mix

I base my marketing strategy on the traditional pillars of marketing. These include - product, price, promotion, and place. I have added four factors - proposal, positioning, people, and potential. When we consider every one of these Ps in relation to PR, we need to add the essential elements of your communication. For example, product relations (PR), promotion relations (PR), potential relations (PR) and so on. This becomes your PR-based marketing strategy.

To understand the process, think of the Ps in your business and how you communicate your reputation through each one. How do you maintain that relationship and trust? For example, how are you communicating your prices to yourself and your stakeholders? Your prices say a lot about where you position yourself as a business. Are you high-end or affordable? What is the language of your promotion? Does your communication style reflect your positioning? Do you reach out to the right places to be seen by those stakeholders? You might want to stop here, write down all the Ps and translate them into PR. This links your PR, marketing, and sales, weaving in your expertise, authority, and trust. Based on your findings, you will need a 'sales script' that gives you guidance when communicating with potential customers.

RETURN ON INVESTMENT (ROI)

 PR is less effective on its own.

 It needs to work in unison with your marketing and sales.

 PR = reputation, credibility and trust.

 MARKETING PR = product, price, promotion, place, proposal, positioning, people and potential.

 SALES PR = all about communication.

 Communications is the thread through them all.

Writing a PR-based sales script

Believing in yourself will impact your sales, which is why it is one of my key performance indicators (KPIs). One of the most important things you can do for your business is to understand how PR, marketing, and sales work together harmoniously. The result is newsworthy marketing, reputation-building content, and pillars of communication that lead to gaining clients, and as a result, your start-up business can flourish. Scaling your business requires ingenuity; making one small change can make all the difference without costing you a penny.

One thing I could have done better when I started out was sales, and that is the bottom line. No customers and no sales mean no revenue and no business. That is why fitting your Credibility Confidence into every stage of your sales script can help you get new clients. The effectiveness of your introductory calls is based on your authority, expertise, and ability to gain trust. Sales representatives use sales scripts to ensure they say the right things to prospective customers during sales interactions. Providing thought-provoking information and a supportive relationship establishes you as a trusted adviser. You need to have enough faith in your offer to prevent them from going to your competitor. If you have Credibility Confidence, your potential customers will believe in you too.

Sales scripts can take many forms, ranging from a detailed word-for-word script to a short list of key talking points. Your sales script may be based on a discussion that follows this list.

1. Your confidence to decide the ideal product or service your prospective client needs
2. Your expertise in the challenges, issues, and competition they face

3. How you confidently sell the benefits because you know what they need
4. The skill you have to link their problems to your benefits
5. The depth of the thoughtful, considered, and insightful questions you ask
6. The level of belief that you have that your solution is the best
7. How you behave as a consultant who doesn't need to talk but listen
8. The ability to say, "This is what you need" as an authority and gain trust
9. To know that you have earned their time or business
10. Your ability to communicate all of the above to your target customers

The best sales process is backed up by excellent customer service. It's crucial to your business that you are available to potential and existing customers. How you and your employees respond to their needs, feelings, and attitudes will build the loyalty and trust you need when you cannot provide a quality service. If you can become a great communicator, you will leave a good impression on your customers, provide valuable information, give personalised service, and actively listen to their concerns. Good customer service skills such as these are free PR and will allow you to solve problems quickly and efficiently. It is best to keep responses to customer questions concise and clear without leaving out any critical details. Great customer service is one way to deliver on your 'service promise.' Your reputation depends upon it.

Why your PR relies on delivering your 'service promise'

Your service promise is a tangible way for customers to experience your brand and know what to expect. It includes how you will interact with them in order to be consistent throughout their customer journey. There is a thread of PR in every aspect of your customer services with your prospects and customers based on your service promise. Buyers expect more than just a consistent flow of relevant content and conversations that add value to their lives in today's world. They want help moving down the path toward their goals. Moreover, when they have achieved those goals, they want to feel confident that your company will continue to support them when they need it most. Don't forget to fact-check to get the best results for the audience; transparency and being open and honest with customers creates solid relationships and collaboration.

By providing a 'service promise' and communicating it to customers, you can boost your reputation for delivering quality products and services. If you provide a service promise but fail to deliver on that promise, you are doing yourself a disservice because your reputation relies on you keeping it. Your PR is one way to make that service promise and communicate it to your customers; your customer service needs to back up that promise by delivering the service you describe in your PR. There are some essential elements of your services promise that can be communicated in your PR and marketing, including:

- What you offer to customers
- The delivery of your product or service
- How your team provides consistency in that delivery
- The reason your prospective customers should choose you
- How you differentiate your offer from competitors' offers
- Your unique product or service that meets their needs

Can your start-up scale the quality of your customer service?

As your business grows, one way to become more accessible is to leverage technology and improve your customer experience. Technology can make you more responsive to your customers in their time of need. When you take on employees, they need to understand your business, know your service promise, and feel valued in a way that they want to satisfy customers and enjoy their work, meaning you will be able to provide better customer service. When people care about the quality of their work and know how to meet their customers' needs promptly, they respond quickly to complaints and problems. Social listening and monitoring will allow you to engage with your customers in real-time.

Your PR strategy can eventually be woven into how you interact with your potential and existing customers. Web Chats, Bots for repeated questions and answers, and video conversations are examples of how technology can help improve customer service. Self-service consumer relationships such as providing Frequently Asked Questions (FAQ), online discussion forums, interactive diagnosis and virtual assistants will help manage customer support issues before they reach the point of contact with a human agent.

Having systems in place for your service channels, such as a Customer Relationship Manager (CRM), can help you quickly work out where your customers are in their journey and provide vital information for the marketing and sales teams. You need to be accountable for any reason your customer process needs to be fixed. What do you need to change to make it more successful? How can you adapt it to provide more consistency, a better understanding of customer needs and more responsive service? How does this improve your customer experience, the relationship, and how your customers and other stakeholders view you?

PR becomes an essential part of your growth strategy when you scale a business. Something a little extra I learned about PR and getting in the PR game is that it is a gift that keeps on giving. Here is another non-exhaustive list to get you thinking about what is in store for you and your business.

14 ways PR can help you think bigger and make more money

- Investment
- New market sectors
- Attracting employees
- Expansions and mergers
- Diversifying
- Increased productivity
- Increase turnover
- Develop new products
- Up-selling
- Charging more
- Reducing competition
- Impressing stakeholders
- Awards
- Increased efficiency

PR messages tailored to various learning and communication needs

If you want to be effective at PR, you need to consider your audience's communication needs. Each individual human has their own way of understanding and perceiving the world. Therefore, it is so hard for us to agree on everything. It is true in person and in the written word. The way you convey your ideas and information will determine how your message is received and how the recipient acts on the information. Remember that communication consists of exchanging thoughts, not just words but with images, sounds or even hand gestures. People communicate in numerous ways, so you can use these multiple mediums to reach out to new audiences with a consistent message.

Knowing where to focus your efforts in a world with so many different communication styles takes work. Some of my clients have Attention deficit hyperactivity disorder (ADHD), Dyslexia or English as their second language. I have written content at the charity in easy-read or 'Plain English' and interviewed non-verbal people. Plain English is a style of writing that uses simple words, short sentences, and everyday language. It avoids jargon and rarely uses acronyms. Plain English wording is intended to be suitable for almost anyone and allows for good understanding to help readers know a topic.

Through communication, we can share unique thoughts to inspire, motivate, and teach others. This is what I call 'Connecting Different Dots' when we make leaps from one idea to another that create new avenues of thinking. If you struggle to get your ideas into a format you feel comfortable with, it is essential to find someone you relate to who can help you unravel your thoughts and show them back to you, so you see them yourself with pride. Increasingly artificial intelligence (AI) is also helping us to master the process of sharing information too.

There is a bonus to asking yourself why you are creating communications. "So what?" is a question we should all ask ourselves at every step of our customer journey. I have often worked with clients who want to share an insight but haven't considered why they are sharing it. It is also a relevant question considering how short our attention spans have become. Many of us live a life of constant distraction where we are always on the go, and even when we make time to focus, we get side-tracked by our devices and social media. It is not just journalists that need a good hook these days.

To make more money, focus on making time as your currency

We have so much more time starting out in business because we have fewer customers. Time is our currency as a start-up. It allows us to work out what media is best for us. It sounds like a lot to contend with initially, but outsourcing your PR and marketing requires funding

155

you may still need to achieve. Using your own expertise as part of your media strategy is free. You've got an edge over your competitors if you take a grassroots approach and get to know your audience on a deeper level. It is the most effective way for you to establish credibility, so you can build trust with your customers now and then learn to scale your business with Credibility Confidence.

Your compelling start-up story is the key to scaling

Maybe my 'people pleaser' personality makes me love PR. It could be the warm memory of my mother at the school she worked at as she talked about its history, recent qualification statistics, and architecture to guests and visitors, who listened intently to everything she said. It may be my role as a mediator in my own family; I relied on communication and negotiations to keep everyone happy. Whatever the reason, I now negotiate between clients and journalists using the same skills.

When I graduated with my Postgraduate certificate in 2011, I walked back down the aisle of Coventry Cathedral with a head full of knowledge but without the skillset to use it and share it. It took me years to return to study for my CIPR Professional PR Diploma because I needed to implement what I had learned rather than learning more and 'overthinking'. "Is it my education or experience in PR that makes me different?" I ask myself. I realise now it is the latter.

This is my backstory; what is yours? How compelling is it? Does it create a solid foundation for your vision of a successful future business?

News stories that go viral - how they can happen

Recently I discovered the power of a news story going viral, and to be honest, it was terrifying. I felt like I was playing 'Whack-a-mole' as the media attention began to escalate. Every time there was a new interest in the story, I needed to reassess and rely on a flexible strategy. I felt every moment along with my client as the story was syndicated globally and was translated into many languages on the way. Syndication is where journalists share stories with other media, and this was one of those stories. This was a learning curve for me as an empath because I could feel that newsroom tension even over the phone. I had seen viral stories before but had never been in the thick of it. What a lesson! Getting in the PR game can skyrocket your visibility. For tips on how to harness that impact, reread Chapter 5.

When it is smarter to lay low as a start-up

There are a lot of benefits to staying under the radar as a start-up, including avoiding overexposure. Being featured in mainstream media can be exhausting and overwhelming, and it doesn't always pay off. Laying low is like 'pause'; it maintains the clarity of your message and coordinated consistency across all channels, including local press and all forms of online media. It's also smart to leave enough time for people to digest your message. This way, you can create maximum impact and avoid negative publicity.

Let's go back to crises: SWOT tactics to stave off PR disasters

Every business is at risk of going through a crisis that could damage its brand's reputation and make them look unprofessional. A crisis could stem from being unprepared or due to a mistake made during the planning process. To avoid this, you must be prepared by establishing your strengths, weaknesses, opportunities, and threats (SWOT) now and in the future. You should review this analysis regularly and make adjustments when necessary.

It's also important to conduct an audit of your business policies and procedures regularly so you are always prepared for events like these. A SWOT analysis not only helps protect against PR disasters, it will also make sure your organisation is not spending or investing money needlessly. I spoke with someone who managed a PR crisis single-handedly with her previous employer. The cost was tens of thousands of pounds in a matter of weeks, so we need to be prepared to overcome disasters with a level of crisis resilience to counteract spending.

Without PR, our marketing and sales become detached from our purpose. The world has changed, the customer has become more sophisticated, and they do not want to feel like they are being sold to. PR and marketing create awareness for your company, your brand and the value of your products and services; it also helps establish credibility. In contrast, sales create revenue by closing the deal with the customer. Clients do not buy from your business; they buy from the person in your business to solve their problems. If you've ever been in sales, then you know how important it is to build trust with the client. PR is just one part of the marketing department, but it can be so much more. It will lead you to Credibility Confidence and increased revenue.

We are going to change the world... together!

With time we gain a potent combination of learned and lived experience. The emotional cost of getting my education almost lost me forever. However, knowing the value of my own lived experience provides an unparalleled sense of achievement. I learned that it was not credentials but Credibility Confidence that empowers us to unlock our expertise with purpose. I am not at the end of my journey as a PR professional, but I've learned some valuable insights that can help you to move forward. That success is what I want for you too.

I would like to see more people like you being rewarded for their achievements and reaching their potential. It is important that we don't always rely on others' approval but instead use it to springboard a belief in ourselves as we see ourselves through another lens. Many people have immense expertise they could share and help others with, but they don't feel it is worthwhile. Many of us experience imposter syndrome these days, but if we all become emotional cheerleaders for each other, we can get past our self-doubt and dare to dream, strive to be the best version of ourselves and have the faith to make our dreams a reality.

CHAPTER 11

Maintaining Your Energy and Focus

Measure Your PR Successes with Facts and Figures

A key part of the PR process is determining what you want to achieve, which will be unique to your needs. When starting out in business, we have a blank canvas for creating our future brand. My biggest tip is to have a strategy, even if that is just in your mind's eye because you need to continue as an expert in what you do, whatever happens in the future. Integrity, for example, is a value and way of life rather than simply a brand statement. As I have mentioned, one thing I notice regularly is that people tend to overshare when they're starting out; they don't realise everything they say in the media can stay there forever and haunt their reputation. Sometimes it's tempting to fall into the trap of telling your entire life story; as I have already suggested, only tell the media the part of your story that is relevant to what you want them to remember about you.

Oversharing leaves me with a challenge when I meet clients who are victims of this. It's essential for us to think about the impact of our stories on others, especially when we're talking about our own vulnerabilities that may not be relevant to our business goals. When authenticity becomes part of your strategy though, it can positively impact how customers view you, especially if you're being transparent with them about what's going on in your life. For me, there is a big difference between positive authenticity and the negative effects of vulnerability. This is one of the most challenging parts of my role as a PR professional.

How to Use Key Performance Indicators to Maximise Your ROI

PR is all about context. We can be authorities in many areas of our lives, so it's critical to remain relevant to the topic and stay focused on your PR message. You could end up down a rabbit hole, struggling to recover. Although most people fear public speaking, it can help you become confident both in person, in written contributions, and on social media. Finding your voice, the one you are most comfortable with when engaging with your audience and customers - not hesitating for words that last for milliseconds to those listening - helps you when it matters most. Remember, confidence breeds credibility.

So what are your goals in PR right now, and how will you measure your success? What are your key performance indicators (KPIs)? A KPI is quantifiable and measures performance over time for a specific objective, providing targets for teams to shoot for, milestones to gauge progress, and insights that help you and your employees make better decisions.

While every business wants to achieve a positive outcome from its PR efforts, not all media channels offer the same kind of return on investment (ROI). Integrating all promotional media with PR can create a formula with clearer metrics to measure success and important KPIs that any business can use to track progress.

Although measuring the impact of implied endorsement from your PR activities is difficult, Little PR Rock Marketing has developed a benchmarking system to address this challenge. Measurement of media coverage should be based on business results and goals. Media monitoring, research and analysis can demonstrate how your brand message is received by its audience and how this affects its know, like, and trust factor. Earned media is a tactic, not an objective. Goodwill, or the positive effect a business's name has on its stakeholders, is affected by the lifespan of the information associated with your brand name. When your image is used on a magazine cover or in other forms of media without any effect, I think of it as 'vanity publishing'.

Are you considering these 5 Key ROI Marketing Principles?

If you can remember as far back as Chapter 1, I have devised five key areas where I measure my success in PR, and I refer to them weekly to help me stay motivated. Even though some of these measurements may not be financial, investing in PR is more important than ever. Do not focus on how you are perceived in the present at the expense of your future reputation. Your audience will decide your credibility based on how well you adapt and react to your environment. These are my Five Key ROI Marketing Principles for my own PR, which include Respect, Recognition, Reputation, Resilience and Reinforcement.

PR & MARKETING PRINCIPLES

5 KEY ROI ©

1 RESPECT

2 RECOGNITION

3 RESILIENCE

4 REPUTATION

5 REINFORCEMENT

CREDIBILITY CONFIDENCE: How to Leverage PR as a Start-Up.

Keep this list for reference as it explains my ROI elements in more detail. These are the summary of the elements that have been covered into a memorable concept. It is the kind of 'Connecting Different Dots' that gets you noticed.

Respect

What effect does respect have on you? If you think of being featured in the media, being asked to speak at an event and being asked for your commentary as a subject-matter expert, you feel a sense of satisfaction like no other. Reflecting on what makes you unique and what you stand for is central to how your audience and clients see you. Your ideas and concepts are also so important.

You need to be aligned with your achievements, abilities, and qualities if you want to gain respect from others. That is why respect is one of my Five Key ROI Marketing Principles. I promote myself by reflecting respect in how I promote myself to others, including my clients, audience, and others in my own industry. Being respected boosts your self-esteem, which gives you the incentive to strive for more.

Recognition

How do you feel about being in the spotlight in a credibility feature that relies on you for your opinion? Standing on a stage and being heard for what you value most in business? Being recognised by your peers for being great at what you do is priceless. You're an expert; the media wants to interview you. There are many ways to get recognition, but media coverage is an indirect endorsement that can make a massive difference. Everyone is wary about marketing, but seeing you featured or asked to speak will give them a reason to trust you.

Remember, there are two ways to reach the media: You can find them directly, through research, your connections or as I do with a database (which can be challenging), or they can find you through media request subscription services and social media.

Resilience

A backup plan for your 'earned media' is important to resilience. Resilience is about flexibility, problem-solving and self-awareness. It means being able to respond quickly and bounce back from setbacks. To compliment earned media, you need to include your social media channels, website, blogs, brochures, email marketing and so forth This is where you are ultimately in charge of your content and backing up your ideas, concepts, and message. In this way, you can trial and demonstrate your thought leadership in your shared industry insights and announce news and information.

Resilience is one of my five key principles for marketing ROI because when it works in harmony with clarity, your message is more effective. Journalists and editors may look for your online channels to discover more about you before deciding whether to add your contribution to their publications. As already mentioned, resilience is also like Teflon, which acts as a protective coating and allows rejection to slide off you.

Reputation

Your reputation is the most important part of your business, both professionally and personally. Your reputation will follow you, whether you like it or not. Your reputation is how people will remember you in the future. If people trust you and believe in what you do, it can make a big difference in your life path. Your reputation is built on how well you communicate with your stakeholders. One way to have consistent exposure is to create graphics that represent your brand well. With repeated opportunities to promote yourself as "As Seen In", your reputation by association can become well-known enough to set you apart from your competition. Your reputation is what people remember about you when you are not there. Your reputation can be the thing that sets you apart from your competition; it may be the only thing.

Reinforcement

To be successful in PR and marketing, you need to be able to choose your channels and share your message consistently. Part of your marketing strategy needs to reassure people that you are reinforcing what you do in the media and your content marketing. When you are consistent, it helps people to associate you with a clear contribution to your industry and them as your customers and audience. It will help them to remember what you say, reinforce your message with clarity and remind them of you when they hear similar content and subjects. There is a skill in saying the same things in many ways, which I can help you with. You can do this by looping an audience through all your media and stressing your values and opinion-based content. Reinforcement is one of my Five Key ROI Marketing Principles because it creates the environment that your online and face-to-face presence sits within.

Benchmarking is a crucial strategic marketing tool

Benchmarking is one part of my strategy that will define your goals, decide which metrics you use, extract your data, and help you to share your expert brand story. It is vital to continue to monitor your statistics as they fluctuate depending on the environment. Although benchmarking is usually used as a crisis management tool, I use brand filters and align them with the KPIs.

When we review the customer journey, it plays a big part in your business strategy. It enables you to measure and monitor what people are saying about you and your brand. Although nothing can be guaranteed, understanding what you want your customers to say about you and what they are saying about you is crucial to your PR measurement and future strategy. Questions to ask yourself include: How do you reassure your clients that you will provide them with the proper guidance and stability? Are you known for your commitment to excellence, and do you provide excellent service on a regular basis? How are you creating an environment where your employees and freelancers can learn, grow, and feel valued? Are you sharing resources and solutions with other members of your community?

The achievement benchmarks that I measure and monitor for Little PR Rock Marketing I update in a simple spreadsheet. You can select the ones that are most relevant to your business and focus on those as a starting point. This spreadsheet is one of your free resources to sign up for, so just follow the instructions coming soon.

Respect:

- Authority building
- Guest articles
- Guest blogs
- Quotes used

Recognition:

- Media coverage
- Trade publications
- Mentions and shout outs
- Social media engagement
- Collaborations
- Domain authority (DA)

Resilience:

- Continuous Professional Development (CPD)
- Gained email connections
- LinkedIn profile view
- LinkedIn searches
- Quality leads
- Sales
- Increased contacts
- Increased followers
- Phone calls
- Google audit
- Google review
- Further opportunities

Reputation:

- Go-to expert status
- Business brand building
- Referrals
- Testimonials
- Customer reviews
- Backlinks

Reinforcement:

- Return on Investment (financial)
- Strategy effectiveness
- Positive impact
- Employer satisfaction (for those still employed)

These are direct examples of how your media works harmoniously to create measurable results. When I was featured in the local newspaper for writing this book, they shared the article on social media; then there was the link to the pre-order page on my website; the same press release was shared in various business magazines online, within the Chamber of Commerce in print and online, I was then asked to appear on radio and so on. The result is that this one topic created a buzz that led to various further opportunities and, in the process, clients too.

I have also worked on prize giveaways with national magazine competitions where this process enables data capture, which immediately creates a response for others looking for that ability to be seen in those magazines and collect opt-in details for subscribers. By demonstrating your credibility and success, as in Chapter 5, it is possible to create an immersive environment of your expertise, taking people from one media to another.

Is PR the secret weapon to your business success?

PR is a bedrock of business. We know we need it, but we don't really know why. If we think about it too hard, it will start to give us a headache. The truth is that PR is everywhere, and its value can't be ignored. PR is central to all your daily activities, from getting a job to selling products and services to building your personal brand. The most interesting part about the concept of PR is that you do not have to be a professional to understand it; in fact, you already use it every day without even knowing it. PR is at the core of how people perceive you and your business; your ability to influence others impacts every aspect of your life.

Why PR is a dirty word (and how to fix that)

So why is PR still looked down upon? It might be because so many people do it poorly. If you're willing to invest in the right kind of training and education, you can elevate yourself above your competition with PR. This book will help you to earn media coverage using proven tactics I have used myself as a PR start-up after ten years of positioning the charity I worked for as thought leaders and innovators.

To be successful, we have to work with journalists and editors who are always under the gun, dealing with multiple deadlines for stories and trying to get information (or 'exclusives') that will make their publication stand out from the rest of the crowd. The best PR comes from understanding what makes a great story and knowing how to pitch it; that means showing up on time, being well-prepared, and having your facts straight.

Your future reputation needs you to gain Credibility Confidence

PR is the ideal marketing fit for your start-up to develop your future reputation. Ask yourself what you really know about public relations so far. It's a diverse field, so knowing how PR works could be the difference between a successful campaign and another failed attempt. While there are many different types of public relations (corporate, crisis, etc.), this book focuses on how PR can help your start-up gain more visibility, credibility, and trust in your industry.

As a start-up, one of the most important things you can do early on is to establish yourself as a credible expert in your space. Just like building any relationship, gaining credibility requires time, effort, and consistency. Most importantly, it requires that you take action every day to make it happen. The best way to build credibility is by applying daily PR tactics like the ones in this book and maintaining a strategic approach to getting media attention for your brand or company. If you want to be successful with PR as part of your marketing program, there is no time like the present.

We are all media experts in some way. The only difference is that some of us have been given the spotlight and others have yet to. We

171

all have a story to tell, but we must be taught how to share it in a manner that is captivating and effective. This requires a shift in mindset from focusing on our marketing message to genuinely focusing on how we can impact others with our expertise. Holding yourself back from your aspirations is one of the biggest mistakes you can make. The reality is that the world needs you. Everyone has a unique perspective and something to offer, and your readers and audience want your expertise. I know that might sound a little grandiose, but it's true.

Stop. Now start with your answers to these questions

When it comes to media, there are two questions to consider; what do you want to comment about, and what types of media do you want to be featured in? Those two questions are really tightly related because if you're interested in a certain topic, the chances are good that others are too, and someone out there may be trying to keep up with the latest trends in your field. If you can write an article on a popular subject and get it published on a highly-trafficked site, that's great exposure for you and the subjects you are discussing. Remember, it could influence people's perceptions about another related issue.

Here are some further questions to ask yourself now.

What do you want to be known for? If you're an expert in your field, think about what makes your knowledge unique. Is it something you learned from experience? Something you were taught? Or is it simply that you've been providing your services for a long time and are now so immersed in the subject matter that it's become part of who you are? If you could be quoted, what would you want to say? What would your expert insights be that set you apart from your competition? What relevant background story of your life brings authenticity to your expertise? How do you impact others with your expertise? Are you entertaining and funny, or are there things about your personality that make people feel comfortable around you and help them with hard conversations about stressful topics? Do you break down otherwise complicated ideas into terms they can understand and apply to their lives?

Essential tips for developing your PR research and curation

One way to begin is by making a list of potential topic titles for articles you could contribute and predicting the questions the media will ask you about these topics. Create catchy titles and write 5-10 bullet points underneath to entice people to read on. Then break each bullet point into three sections. The first section should be a relevant backstory; the second should contain top tips and insights to support your opinion; the third should be a call to action encouraging your audience to do something related to your commentary. This process can also be done with various tools designed to spark ideas, then collect and organise them, which can help you to generate creative ideas while making decisions. Remember not to underestimate the power of research and only use artificial intelligence tools in content creation when you get a mental block. We all get stuck, and sometimes we need a little help to get started.

FREE RESOURCES

To access your free resources, please email me and let me know the following:
- How you got your copy of this book
- Which chapter is your favourite and why?
- The page number with your top takeaway
- To Whom would you recommend this book?

Please use the subject line:
CC BOOK Reader: FREE RESOURCES

abbi@littleprrockmarketing.co.uk
www.littleprrockmarketing.co.uk
(+44) 07966 712017

CHAPTER 12

Your Expert Breakthrough

Get Your Story Out There to Those Who Need It

PR: The complementary ingredient in a successful marketing mix

Investing in PR and marketing can be expensive, and many think it's pointless or even detrimental to their bottom line. In today's highly commoditised 'buyer's market,' it seems there is no way to differentiate oneself from the competition, so why bother investing in marketing at all? We are all bombarded with promotional messages by businesses trying to sell us their products or services. Most of these messages are targeted at the buyer's logical side, the part that makes decisions based on facts and figures.

On their path toward a purchase, buyers rarely hear about the emotional reasons why they should choose one product over another. This is where PR comes in. A good PR campaign helps create buzz about your company, its products, and its brand through traditional media (newspapers, magazines), blogs, social media platforms and other outlets that reach potential customers, but not as an advertisement or sales pitch.

The last thing anyone wants is for something bad to happen because someone didn't do their PR homework and plan ahead for the worst-case scenario. This book can help to position you as an authority, go-to expert and thought leader, but I cannot guarantee results. The hard work comes from you, so have a plan for both positive and negative results.

One of the most powerful steps in positioning yourself as an expert is writing a book like this. Writing a book isn't for everyone. It's not just a resume; it's a place where you can share your ideas and insights more deeply. But, for many people like me, it's hard to get started on writing a book. You will know the right time to write a book if that is your goal because you will feel that you will burst if you don't download all the information to help that one person who needs to hear it.

You might put it off, but you will know that you need to do it now. Do not take the easy way out and try to get someone else to write your book for you because you can always make notes for a ghost-writer like me to string together. It is your book, and there are only so many books that can be written about a subject before it is over-saturated and no one wants to read about that subject anymore. I have seen authors who are willing to pay other people to write their books for them, which means they need to be more passionate about their message to deliver it themselves. If authors truly believe in their message, then they deserve to master it in their own communication style and with their own voice.

So what is stopping you from doing PR right now?

Fear?

Doubt?

Procrastination?

Self-sabotage?

Imposter-syndrome?

Ridicule?

I have felt all of the above and survived, as you will too. One thing I do know is that you will only know if you try. By trialling your expertise with the media, you get to research your industry more often, stay ahead of the curve and see what matters most. This process will be exciting if you are genuinely passionate about what you do. If not, you may be in the wrong expertise field. That simply means finding something else you are good at or, alternatively, deciding that PR with thought leadership marketing is not for you and your business at this time.

Remember, PR is not a sales-generating machine you can turn on to get clients. It has its place but will not replace relationship-building and traditional sales tactics. There are times when you will need to focus on the different promotional areas of your business because, without sales, there is no business revenue. However, if you're reading this book, you've probably figured out that PR is an important part of your start-up, but it might not be clear what exactly that means to you yet. Before making any decisions, take some time to reflect on how PR can benefit you and your business based on what you know now.

THE AIDA MODEL

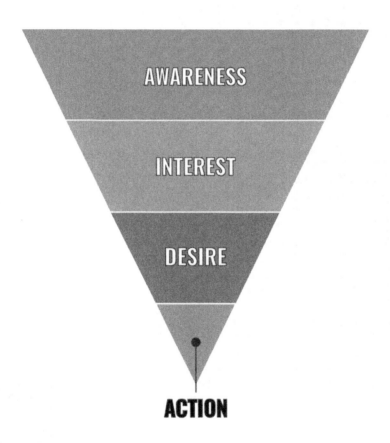

AWARENESS

INTEREST

DESIRE

ACTION

How to make PR AIDA Model work for you

Here are some ideas that could help you based on The AIDA Model, which stands for Attention, Interest, Desire, and Action model. This advertising effect model identifies the stages a customer goes through during a purchasing decision. This is my PR adaptation of this process, now called 'The Four Cs of PR AIDA', to get you thinking. Your model might look different to this. When you look at each part of the list, ask yourself, "Where can PR fit in here?"

ATTENTION created through Content:

- newsworthy story
- pitch distribution
- credibility piece
- press release
- book
- build a relationship with the media
- pitch follow-up
- blog/ article
- interview
- social media marketing
- relationship building with media
- slide share
- course created

INTEREST via Communications:

- media coverage
- mention in calls with potential clients
- promote on social media
- add to marketing materials
- include in keynote talks and webinars
- add to your media kit

- add to website
- add PR content to email footer
- create an 'As Seen In' blog
- add media coverage to slide deck
- use text as social media content
- reword for further articles/ contributions
- recorded audio

DESIRE established with Consistency:

- show up in your network
- share media kit everywhere
- pitch the media regularly
- comment and post on social media
- send social media direct messages
- create email connections
- decide follow-up strategy
- email subscription option
- send hyperlink link to website
- share case studies
- send price list
- answer what your stakeholders need
- repurpose content in new ways

ACTION begins with a Call to Action:

- 1-2-1 half-hour discovery call
- prices/ offers given
- quotation sent
- testimonials request sent
- added to email list
- promotional book sent
- directed to PR training
- signposted to articles online and in print

- phone number exchanged
- social media connected
- request follow-up date

As a start-up, you can take a basic idea and turn it into a success by providing creativity, flair, and professionalism to help your PR make the required impact. You can do this through a PR campaign. A PR campaign is just a series of planned activities that all have a specific purpose and work toward the same business goal. It sounds complex, but for now, think simple and effective. Do not try to be too clever with PR stunts, spin, and events; just think about what you have already. That is your expertise and how you will tell your truth. So, for example, every one of the tactics on this list could be a PR campaign activity on a small scale.

How to plan and execute a PR campaign on a modest budget

The activities involved in a PR campaign vary depending on the objective and goals of the campaign, but PR campaigns always have an objective and usually have a fixed time frame. Many businesses turn to professionals for assistance with PR campaigns, and you will, too, when you can afford to. I understand how difficult it is to do your own PR because I've done my own. A press release and pitch that might take me a few hours for a client once took me several to create for myself. The feelings of fear, doubt, and procrastination creep in, and I sympathise with my clients who struggle to master their own content. Perhaps the most embarrassing part of that admission is that I am a PR professional, and it happens to me too. You are not alone.

If you are a start-up business, you probably have an inquisitive mind and perhaps love to experiment and take risks like me. You may be eager to get started on your PR research. You may want to make that list of where you'd like to be featured; plan ahead with PR campaigns for the next 90 days, six months, or even a year. Remember to test and report on everything as you go so you can learn your own strategies. It is a good thing to be nervous before tinkering with your reputation.

You may still be wondering how you can be expected to write newsworthy content. The truth is anyone can write something newsworthy if they know how to cover all the bases and do it right. Why not go through a newsworthy list again? You can choose the one that resonates with you and write down five key topics, the sub-topics that I mentioned of relevant personal stories, your soundest expertise, and your call to action.

Every thought leader, expert, and authority comment you make should excite you and make you anxious, just like when I spoke in front of my PR peers. What are your glitches? What are the things you must not say that are just waiting to jump out of your mouth? When writing articles, blogs, and opinion pieces, check everything and double-check again just to make sure. If you miss something, have your apology statement at hand. If you want to get through a bad situation in PR, the best way is to come clean about it. The most effective method of dealing with an issue is: to be honest and open up about it. I've learned that the best defence against a PR crisis is honesty. You can wear honesty for any occasion and radiate with authentic vulnerability without selling your soul for one-sided media coverage.

Your start-up's biggest news is waiting for PR - what will you do?

As we have established, newsworthiness is essential for PR; if your start-up's news is familiar, why should anyone care? So, how do you know when you have something significant for the journalist or producer? The answer is that there is a burning desire to get it out of

182

your system. PR pros are trained to keep a tight lid on their projects because they know the value of having a story leak out before it's ready. Think of a time when you had to hold a secret. Maybe it was a surprise party, or your partner had planned something special for you. Now, imagine that instead of just holding that information in, you were forced to stay silent about it. As much as we might want to reveal the juicy details of what we're working on behind the scenes, it's not in our best interest to do so. Releasing that secret at the right time is key to good PR.

Now that you have the PR know-how I used to gain credibility and a reputation, you can do the same thing so that your clients find you. That's because you now know as much as I did when I created my own Credibility Confidence. If you use this information wisely, you'll be able to write, speak, create visual content, and contribute your expertise with caution.

Why do I say, "with caution"? My experience is that if you get complacent, PR mistakes could quickly occur. So, start by doing research both inside and outside of your business. The book you are reading is an example of how I did that to gather insights that I remember helped me. The stories within this book are my experience backed up with research so that they are as accurate as possible and not biased advice. It took me a year and a half to compile all the information I needed, but now I know I can go to the next level in my business. You can gain Credibility Confidence, too, because you saw something in your new business that could create a new way of life for you. Let others see it too!

If you want better media coverage, you need to feed journalists better information

The truth is that hundreds of thousands of business owners and entrepreneurs would happily share their stories and help journalists write better articles, build a clearer picture, and give a more balanced opinion. As business owners, we have a part to play in feeding back to journalists on what they report and providing a direct line for journalists to get the real facts they need. We have the power to change what we see in the media by working together and feeding back the truth of our stories through media channels.

The media can seem intimidating, but most journalists are just looking for stories their readers will be interested in. Credibility Confidence will change your perspective, help you overcome your fears and help you see that the media are not a big, faceless mass of power that can dole out praise or reputation punishment at will. What reporters want most is a good story that their readers will be interested in, and if you have a fascinating story to tell, there's no reason your interaction with the press should be anything but positive. Reporters are just like regular people doing a job, if you can give them something newsworthy, everyone wins.

Set goals and rewards to get out there and unlock the power of your PR

The work you have been putting in to understand and explore the world of PR is now a tool in your hands. You now know what you need to be planning to get the attention of the people who need to see your awesomeness. You've read my stories and taken away some information from them, so I hope they have inspired you. Do reread any areas where you need clarification to start your PR journey. Now, take it further. Don't just remember what I told you; put it into action. The best way to make sure you will do it is to set goals for yourself with deadlines and rewards.

Think about how much better your life could be when more people are paying attention to what you want them to pay attention to, i.e. you, your business, your brand, your product, and your service. Be inventive, creative, and out of the box; drive your next PR campaign because that's what this book is about, being on top of the media by understanding it and using strategies to help you to gain Credibility Confidence. Once you know where you are going, start planning and implementing your strategy.

Go ahead. Make the headlines. Make an impact. Make an income.

CHAPTER 13

Bonus Chapter: Communications Change

No, 'revishock' is not a word. I created it

Just when you thought reading this book had ended, the page turns, and the text springs back to life with yet more to say. You may feel the full impact of what I call 'revishock!' This is the blended word (or portmanteau) that I have chosen to describe this resurrection phenomenon. It blends the words 'revitalise' and 'shock.' Think of new words such as selfies, anti-vaxxers, chillaxing, photobombing, mansplaining, bromances, flashmobs, crowdfunding, sexting, greenwashing, partygate or the gig economy. The way you use language could be the vital aspect of your pitch that gets you noticed by a journalist or editor. A neologism is a new word, expression, or meaning in a language that catches on in the media and eventually becomes part of our dictionaries. Revishock is my latest neologism just for you; it is 'hot off the press' as I write this. What is yours?

More seriously, the words of journalists and other writers have often moved the world. The rise of journalism as an art form is often linked to the flair of the journalist faced with a fast-approaching deadline. According to my sources, 'Weapons of Mass Destruction' (WMD) first appeared as a phrase in The London Times in 1937. The term 'Cold War' was coined in 1947 by journalist Herbert Bayard Swope of the New York World in speeches for Bernard Baruch.

In November 2022, Collins Dictionary's choice of 'permacrisis' for Word of the Year felt about right, given the state of the world at the time. The term 'quiet quitting also entered the Collins list of 10 words or phrases that "reflect our ever-evolving language and the preoccupations of those who use it" for that year. Quiet quitting refers to employees who carry out their basic duties at work and no more, either out of protest or to improve work/life balance.

The Oxford Dictionaries, on the other hand, announced its first Word of the Year for 2022, chosen by public vote, as 'goblin mode', which describes a state of being that is unapologetically self-indulgent, lazy, slovenly, or greedy. 2022 was a great year for words that describe the state of being in extreme anxiety caused by the financial uncertainty of living through a period of war, inflation, and political instability. Where there is a story, an article or commentary, there are new words that could be used. We need to find them to communicate our story to others.

It's not just words that impact your audience in isolation. It may be a phrase that stands the test of time. Creating a memorable phrase could make you "as happy as Larry." Laurence 'Larry' Foley was an undefeated champion Australian boxer during the 19th century. In the 1870s, he reportedly won the Australian championship in a bare-knuckle boxing bout, winning a vast sum. A New Zealand newspaper apparently used the phrase "as happy as Larry" when referring to the throngs of people celebrating the win. The saying is still used today in New Zealand, Australia, and Britain: one fight, one phrase. Pick your battles with wordsmithery, and you could be the next Larry.

There are some great references to follow in the References to appreciate this book further and learn more. Learning is a gift, so remember to share your insights too.

ABBI E. HOXLEIGH PGCert MCIPR

PR & COMMUNICATIONS STRATEGIST

MARKETING WITH PERSEVERANCE & RESILIENCE

Areas of Expertise:

- Thought Leadership
- Entrepreneurship
- Public relations
- Marketing
- Communications

Available For:

- Keynotes
- Consultations
- Workshops
- PR services
- Marketing services

CONTACT DETAILS

abbi@littleprrockmarketing.co.uk
www.littleprrockmarketing.co.uk
(+44) 07966 712017

EPILOGUE

As we come to the end of this book, I hope you have found it to be a valuable resource for building a successful start-up with the help of PR. I want to encourage and advise you in a way that makes PR easy to understand. If you are reading this and thinking, "I want to get started working on my PR. Let me loose," as a start-up or a more established business, then I have done my job. It's never too late for you to start.

Through this book, I have shared my knowledge and experience to demonstrate to you--the reader--that I am walking the talk. I have left no stone unturned, sharing my highlights, mistakes, and PR's pros and cons to help you master your reputation with Credibility Confidence.

As a start-up founder or entrepreneur, I know adapting to change is crucial. PR is now essential to get heard and gain credibility in a world saturated with noisy communications. I hope you have found the format and layout of this book easy to navigate, with infographics and visuals supporting your understanding of the content.

Thank you for choosing Credibility Confidence as your guide to mastering PR and confidently building your brand's reputation. Building credibility and establishing a solid reputation takes time and effort, but the payoff is worth it.

If you need any support, let me know at
abbi@littleprrockmarketing.co.uk

REFERENCES

Agility PR (2022). How to Hear a Crisis Coming: 5 Steps for Setting Up Your Media Monitoring Tool for Successful Crisis Detection and Management. [online] Agility PR. Available at: https://www.agilitypr.com/how-to-hear-a-crisis-coming/ [Accessed 4 Oct. 2022]. Downloadable PDF.

Agility PR ed., (2022). 2022 Crisis Comms Mastery Virtual Summit. [Webinar] Available at: https://crisiscommsmastery.com/2022-sessions/ [Accessed 24 Mar. 2022].

Baradell, S. (2021). Earned Media Mastery. [online] Available at: https://earnedmediamastery.com/ [Accessed 5 Jan. 2023].

BBC News. (2022). Permacrisis and Partygate among words of the year. [online] Available at: https://www.bbc.com/news/entertainment-arts-63458467.amp [Accessed 01 Jan 23].

BBC News. (2022). Oxford word of the year 2022 revealed as 'goblin mode'. [online] 5 Dec. Available at: https://www.bbc.co.uk/news/uk-63857329. [Accessed 01 Jan 23].

Behrman, D (n.d.). Free Editorial Coverage in Media/ 3-Step Profitable PR Process. [online] Available at: https://dinabehrman.com/ [Accessed 2022].

Black, C. (2014). The PR professional's handbook : powerful, practical communications. London: Koganpage.

Buday, R. (2022). Competing on Thought Leadership. Kindle ed. Washington D.C.: Idea Press Publishing.

Canfield J. (n.d.). Chicken Soup for the Soul. [online] Available at: https://www.chickensoup.com/.

Crow, M. (2019). Step-by-Step Guide to Outlining a Non-Fiction Book. Available at: https://writingcooperative.com/step-by-step-guide-to-outlining-a-non-fiction-book-13467c9dbc1b [Accessed 14 Aug. 2022].

Dib, A. (2021). 1-PAGE MARKETING PLAN : get new customers, make more money, and stand out from the crowd. S.L.: Page Two Books, Inc.

Dietrich, G. (2020). What Is the PESO Model...and How Do I Use It? [online] Spin Sucks. Available at: https://spinsucks.com/communication/peso-model-breakdown/.

Earned Media Mastery. (2021). Earned Media Mastery. [online] Available at: https://earnedmediamastery.com/ [Accessed 5 Jan. 2023].

Graziosi D. (n.d.). 7 Levels Deep Exercise/ Mastermind.com Inner Circle training. Online Training. [online] Available at: https://www.deangraziosi.com/ [Accessed 5 Jan. 2023].

HuffPost UK. (2015). The Dark Art of Public Relations Goes Legit. [online] Available at: https://www.huffingtonpost.co.uk/alan-edwards/the-dark-art-of-public-re_b_7422120.html [Accessed 5 Jan. 2023].

The Independent. (2022). Opinion: 2022's Words of the Year and what they tell us. [online] Available at:

https://www.independent.co.uk/voices/word-of-the-year-2022-oxford-dictionary-b2254034.html [Accessed 01 Jan 23].

Joy, V. (2019). She Enjoys | Business & Mindset Coaching. [online] Available at: https://she-enjoys.com/ [Accessed 8 Apr. 2022]

Leading Through Crisis. (n.d.). Episode 4 - Interview with Denise Alison. [online] Available at: https://www.leadingthroughcrisis.ca/episodes/denise-alison [Accessed 5 Jan. 2023].

Lyons, B. (2014). The Complete Guide to Using Help A Reporter (HARO). [online] Available at: https://www.brigittelyons.com/haro/ [Accessed 20 Feb. 2021].

Malinchak, J. (2022). Best Seller On Fire. [Webinar] Available at: https://vimeo.com/696257316 [Accessed 4 Apr. 2022].

Moore, S. (n.d.). RockstarPR 2. [online] Available at: https://getrockstarpr.com/ [Accessed 5 Jan. 2023].

muckrack.com. (n.d.). How To Write A Media Pitch: Examples & Best Practices. [online] Available at: https://muckrack.com/media-pitching-guide.

Murphy, D. (2021). How to write a nonfiction book or memoir (free chapter outlining templates). Available at: https://www.creativindie.com/how-to-write-a-nonfiction-book-free-chapter-outlining-templates/ [Accessed 14 Aug. 2022].

pesentation-profits.com. (n.d.). Presentation Profits Virtual Speaker Training. [online] Available at: https://presentation-profits.com/virtual [Accessed 2 Jul. 2021].

Read, S. (2022). Handling the media in a crisis. [Webinar] Available at: https://www.eventbrite.co.uk/e/handling-the-media-in-a-crisis-tickets-330503192947 [Accessed 23 Jun. 2022].

Shout Communications. (n.d.). The 'dark art' of PR dissected. [online] Available at: https://shoutcommunications.co.uk/blog/pr-dark-side-dissected/ [Accessed 5 Jan. 2023].

The Motion Agency. (2022). Public Relations Terminology Helpful PR Definitions. [online] Available at: https://agencyinmotion.com/public-relations-terminology-helpful-pr-definitions/.

The Sow Collective. (n.d.). 10 Tips For a Successful HARO Pitch (With Examples!). [online] Available at: https://www.thesowcollective.com/blog/2018/how-to-write-a-successful-haro-pitch [Accessed 5 Jan. 2023].

tonyrobbins.com. (2016). Unleash The Power Within 2022 Tony Robbins - The Official Website of Tony Robbins. [online] Available at: https://www.tonyrobbins.com/. [4-7 Mar 2021]

Wynne, R. (n.d.). Five Things Everyone Should Know About Public Relations. [online] Forbes. Available at: https://www.forbes.com/sites/robertwynne/2016/01/21/five-things-everyone-should-know-about-public-relations/?sh=5ba729b32a2c [Accessed 9 Jul. 2022].

ACKNOWLEDGEMENTS

Tim Clay – For adapting to me continually changing as a PR professional, public speaker, and author

Susan Stevens – My aunt who always has my back and has seen me flourish

Zoe Jukes – Who listens patiently to my stories and shares my journey as a true cheerleader

Sharon Brown – Who inspired me to write a book in the first instance

The Book Chief Publishing House team – There would be no book without them

Alanna Richards – Her illustration and infographics bring this book to life

Phaedra Elson – Whose illustration of me makes a great portrait

Mark Elson – For being the perfect sounding board for comments as a beta reader

Wendy Brown – Whose ongoing support has enabled me to see myself as a viable business owner

Joanne Parker – Without whom, Chapters 8 and 10 would still be repetitive.

Rachael McNidder – For her thorough and constructive feedback, which empowered me to publish

Debbie Wills – For the synopsis and saying that she didn't want to put down this book.

Kazlina Burroughs – My go-to expert in holding up a mirror to me to see my achievements

Zoe Louise – For listening to my ups and downs as I develop a growth mindset

Danielle Robyn – For bringing together the most impressive book cover graphics

Karen Heap – For introducing me to the networking scene that boosted my confidence as an author

Sandra Garlick MBE – For helping me to find power in my story and a public voice

Roxanna Khanum – For showing me that I am a powerful force to be reckoned with.

Angie Simmons – Whose Sofala Group helped me to focus on writing this book in four weeks

Marcus Grodentz – Who provides unwavering support as PR professional and public speaker

Alistair Driscoll – For the support and for bearing with me as I found the time to dedicate to this book

Vivienne Joy – Who challenges me to be the best version of myself

Jacquie Case – Who has learned along with me as I found my true PR purpose

Kate Findlay – Whose wisdom has guided me and encouraged me not to retire

Adam Walters – The NatWest Accelerator Manager who saw my potential

Chris Tucker – For helping me realise the academic "rigour" needed for my book yet written

Esther Roche – Who provides ideal client content (one of my pitches for her is included)

Datsa Gaile – Whose belief in me as a PR professional goes beyond being a client

Lisa Simcox – Whose advice I value when I feel self-doubt, and I need a pep-talk

Mark Varney and Jo Powell – As a team, they provided my workplace photoshoot

John Cleary – For brilliantly capturing me speaking in public

Ellen Manning - Whose talk about writing for the press motivated me to want to work with journalists

Zoe Bennett - The person who showed me how to put a little 'sass' into my personal brand

APL Media – For the copyright and permission to use my Telegraph advertorial

Doreen Woodward – Who watches from the wings, cheering me on

Annie Johnston – Whose photography makes me look great in headshots now illustrations

AgilityPR – For all the training in PR and the database that keeps me aspiring

Dean Graziosi – For his online Inner Circle lessons in self-education and ethical selling

Tony Robbins – Who transformed my world from employee to business owner during the lockdown

Richard McCann – Whose personal speaking story resonated with me in how to boost my reputation

Jack Canfield – His 'Chicken Soup for the Soul' series inspired the Credibility Confidence series

James Malinchak, Nick, and Megan Unsworth – For their "Best Seller on Fire" free training course

Scott Baradell – For his inspiration to have the PR mindset for thought leadership

Micheal Smart – For the daily PR emails and the acronym DIFT that I use regularly

Alan Dibb – I always refer to the simplicity of his one-page marketing plan

Derek Murphy – For his guide to writing a non-fiction book in thirteen chapters template

ABOUT THE AUTHOR

Abbi E. Hoxleigh was born in Coventry. In Walsgrave Hospital, in fact. Her mother and father are the inspiration for her PR business name Little PR Rock Marketing. Both her parents have passed away, but Abbi knows that somehow and somewhere, they are proud of her. After attending a Rugby High School For Girls, Abbi spent many years at art school and university, where she achieved her Post-Graduate Certificate in Creative Arts at Coventry University, despite years of emotional health concerns with Post Traumatic Stress Disorder (PTSD) and an ever-changing diagnosis that seemed to settle on a Bipolar for many years.

Abbi was determined never to give up on her dreams. (And still doesn't) As a qualified graphic designer, her grasp on communications covers both image and text. She worked for various charities for 21 years after finishing her BA Hons Graphic Design at Wolverhampton University in 2000. Her early experiences in PR were as a marketing volunteer at Walsall Art Gallery in 2000 in its opening weeks and at The Mead Gallery, University of Warwick, where she enjoyed promoting exhibitions.

As an unapologetic learner, Abbi returned to higher education studies several times as a mature student, including her CIPR Professional PR Diploma. She is passionate about mental health as much as she is about communication. She worked as a Graphic Designer, then for several years as a Community Mental Health Assistant at a Rethink Mental Illness recovery house and at a charity supporting women through domestic violence until she finally found her path in media relations in 2011. This cemented her role in PR.

After a brief spell of ill health, and under the guidance of her CEO, Doreen Woodward, at New Directions Rugby Ltd, Abbi flourished as the charity's Media Officer. Abbi received her Post-Graduate Certificate during her years at New Directions and still values the support they gave her for personal growth. In 2018 she started what is now her hobby business designing symbolic jewellery with the help of a computer-aided design (CAD) specialist.

She immersed herself in training from The Chamber of Commerce, Coventry & Warwickshire Local Enterprise Partnership (LEP) Growth Hub, Coventry University Enterprises (CUE), and Socially Shared networking events and received deep structure coaching from her business coach Vivienne Joy until she found Tony Robbins in 2021 and started her PR diploma.

Abbi had been 'unconsciously competent' for years as a media relations professional, and it took the COVID-19 pandemic to unlock her true potential. She had been trialling a graphic design-focused business called The Visuals Adviser since 2020, but 6 months in, she decided her strengths lay in PR. She found her own independence during the pandemic lockdown in 2020, as she worked remotely and made brave decisions. Suddenly she began to soak up business know-how and PR academia like a sponge. It was a time that Abbi reflected on her future, and she knew that if she did not venture out into her own PR business then, she probably never would; she had to try.

When Abbi resigned from New Directions in 2021, she began to gain traction as a PR professional and received support from the NatWest Accelerator and the University of Warwick's Innovation Collective. This was the game changer. However, she still refers to the training she received all those years ago and the businesspeople who have helped her along the way.

So how did Abbi's parents influence her business name? Abbi's mother was called Pauline, which means small or LITTLE. Her father was named Peter, which means ROCK. After remembering Little Rock is actually a location, she decided on LITTLE PR ROCK because her Dad was the family ROCK. She has now become a ROCK for her clients too. Supporting them, nurturing them, and getting them to believe in their own credibility. Her tagline is "With Perseverance and Resilience" -because that is what you need in PR. You need to be Teflon coated and not be offended when things don't go to plan.

Oh, the font she used for PR of her logo in between the two words is ENGAGEMENT. How fitting is that?!

Public Relations Today brings together the best content from hundreds of industry thought leaders. These awards recognise the Most Valuable Posts as judged by their readers, the award committee, machine intelligence and social media. These awards acknowledge the posts that provide the highest value to industry professionals - useful and actionable information that is tactical or strategic in nature, providing either long-term or short-term value.

Pauline and Peter Head.

Printed in Great Britain
by Amazon

21086213R00119